DRAGONS' DEN

DRAGONS' DEN

SUCCESS
FROM PITCH TO PROFIT

Collins

HarperCollins*Publishers*
77–85 Fulham Palace Road
London
W6 8JB

www.collins.co.uk

First published in 2007
This updated paperback edition published in 2008

A catalogue record for this book is available from the British Library.

10 9 8 7 6 5 4 3 2 1

ISBN 978-0-00-727082-8

Designed and typeset by seagulls.net

Printed and bound in Great Britain by Clays Ltd, St Ives plc.

CONTENTS

FOREWORD BY EVAN DAVIS

Dragons' Den was first broadcast on British television in early 2005. The format for the show was imported – with substantial modifications – from Japan.

It was such a simple idea it was surprising that no one had invented it before: entrepreneurs meet a group of investors and pitch their business idea or invention in the hope of securing an investment. Some succeed and walk off with a business partner and tens of thousands of pounds injected into their business. Most fail.

The programme has been more successful than those who were involved in its early production had expected. Few could have predicted just how many interesting characters there are in the business world, or how much drama a televised investment encounter can generate.

The different personalities of the five investors, the 'Dragons', have obviously helped make the show famous, but it's not just about them: the entrepreneurs are a remarkable group of individuals too. They all have enough 'make-it-happen' about them to construct a business plan or a prototype, and for that they deserve our admiration. But some come spectacularly unstuck in the Den, while others just seem to thrive on the atmosphere. Many of them straddle that fine line between genius and insanity.

Quite apart from the personalities, though, there is the drama of watching hopes fulfilled, dreams dashed and over-confidence punished.

The programme is laced with points of tension. From the moment an entrepreneur appears on the stairs, contraption in hand, inviting us to ask what on earth it is that they're holding; to the reaction of the Dragons; to the potential negotiation of a deal. Each stage of the process has its own rules and its own winners and losers.

In essence, *Dragons' Den* takes business on television back to basics. The most important questions about products are not those that you find in the financial section of the newspapers – whether one company will take over another or issue new shares. The most important question is 'will it sell?'

And what's interesting about that question is that any armchair punter can have a point of view: a device for stopping the tap when the bath overflows; a snowbike that puts handlebars on a snowboard; a range of cardboard beach furniture; a device for keeping the tip of a cucumber fresh. You don't have to have any training to be able to ask yourself, would I buy that? Would anyone else buy that? *How much* did you say it costs?

People like me sometimes shy away from calling *Dragons' Den* a 'reality show'. That category is very large, the programmes within it are highly variable and not always very original. I like to think of *Dragons' Den* as being in a class of its own.

Ironically, though, it is actually more realistic than most reality shows, because the deals you see struck on screen are genuine deals and the Dragons actually invest their own money.

It's not scripted and controlled by a team of writers either, so some of the deals you see on screen fail to proceed to completion. Often the entrepreneur subsequently decides not to take up the offer. Sometimes the Dragon and entrepreneur realise they disagree about where the business should go, and part company; sometimes when the Dragons look closely at the business and do their due diligence on the companies they invest in, they find things that simply put them off.

Life's like that.

There's also a certain reality in the fact that the Dragons don't always get it right. There are stories of entrepreneurs who have been turned down by the Dragons going on to bigger things, and entrepreneurs backed by Dragons who ended up struggling.

Business is inherently unpredictable – that's what makes it interesting.

If you have bought this book, you are probably already one of those people who finds business life interesting. If you enjoy the programme as entertainment pure and simple, you can read about the Dragons and some of the entrepreneurs that have taken part.

But you might also be someone who wants to set up your own business. You might be hoping to pitch on the programme. Perhaps even better, you might aspire to be a Dragon yourself.

This book will give you an insight into the kinds of difficult questions that you should ask yourself before embarking on a new career as an entrepreneur, and as *numbers* are the thing that get most people confused, there's a whole chapter on them.

If you are one of those people battling to build a business plan, good luck to you.

I had always felt rather sorry for those entrepreneurs who came into the Den in the first series – they had never been able to watch the programme and see what they were in for. I actually sometimes wondered if we would ever get entrepreneurs to sign up for the later series.

I needn't have worried. The supply has not dried up. There are enough people out there with ideas, courage and the need for investment – and perhaps occasionally a thirst for publicity too – to ensure a steady stream of participants.

It seems *Dragons' Den* was fortunate in emerging just as entrepreneurship became fashionable in Britain.

Unless, of course, it was *Dragons' Den* that *made it* fashionable.

PART 1
MEET THE DRAGONS

W hat makes a Dragon? They all have one thing in common – they have lots of money, and they all made it themselves. So, are the rich different from us? Well actually no, their lives are very similar to ours but with a few key differences. You are about to meet Theo who came to the UK as an immigrant from Cyprus – and by the time he was 20 was already turning businesses around. Duncan was a 'wide boy' with an ice-cream van and a tendency to show people what he really thought of them. He didn't start running a business until he was 30 but his instinct with people is the trademark skill that has made him millions. In contrast, Deborah began her business career when she was seven years old, running a little flower stall outside her house, and now she uses her sales and marketing skills to grow businesses she has invested in. Peter is ultra-competitive and this key business skill has been with him since childhood, always wanting to be top of the class and always massively competitive in his tennis playing. Now he still wants to win, and he uses his innate drive to be the best in his business field of telecommunications both nationally and internationally. James is the new boy on the team – this is the first time you'll get to meet him and hear his story. He is a gentle man who looks after his business like a family, and is excellent at identifying people with entrepreneurial skills and giving them the right opportunity. Richard has left the Den, but his experiences on series three and four have many valuable lessons for us, and he remains part of the Dragons' Den family. His extraordinary rags-to-riches story is one of hard work creating success beyond your wildest dreams, but he has not lost his basic honesty and charm. All our Dragons have their feet on the ground in the real world. Their life stories to date can tell us lots about what it takes to become an entrepreneur.

PETER JONES
THE VISIONARY

Peter Jones was born in 1966 and raised in Berkshire. He attended state schools apart from a couple of terms at a private prep school, and set up his own tennis school at 16. He set up his second business when only just 18 and in his twenties he ran a thriving computer business but through a combination of circumstances he lost the business.

At the age of 28 Peter joined corporate giant Siemens Nixdorf and ran its computer business in the UK. In 1998 he founded Phones International Group, a telecommunications firm that now generates revenues in excess of $250 million.

His business interests include telecommunications, leisure, publishing, property, angel investment as well as TV and media. He is regarded as one of the UK's best-known entrepreneurs.

Peter has won many national awards including The Times/Ernst & Young *Emerging Entrepreneur of the Year in 2002. In 2006 the* Daily Telegraph *listed him as one of the top ten entrepreneurs in the UK aged under 40. Peter is committed to helping more young people*

start their own business and has plans for a Tycoon academy. He spends
a lot of time working with the Government, especially the DTI, helping
to make Britain a more entrepreneurial nation. When you read his
story you will see how much drive an entrepreneur needs to succeed.
Peter's need to win, and desire not to give up, are the business skills that
have made him so successful.

I've always been someone who does what they want to do. I've always been able to make my own decisions from an early age.

My parents sent me to a boys-only private school for a short time when I was seven because they wanted the best for me and they thought that would give me the best chance of a great education. It had a very smart uniform with a cap, blazer, shorts and long socks.

I found it difficult to make the big jump from a state school. I found the whole regime very, very different. It was not so much a lot more strict as more structured and a lot more was expected of you.

I struggled in class – I had done multiplication at a state school, but I was thrown straight in the deep end at my private school, where they were already doing fractions. My reaction was to spend time just trying to understand it. A lot of time at home, a lot of time studying with my dad, trying to work harder.

I was a fish out of water at that school. I made friends but the pupils were different; most of them came from different backgrounds but it just felt strange to me. My main challenge was the lessons, trying to catch up as I was one or two years behind the others, and trying to get back on top. I wanted to be top of the class and that put more pressure on me. I wasn't bottom of the class, but it still wasn't good enough for me. I wanted to be the number one student. I knew that wasn't possible because there were some seriously intelligent boys there. I remember it now, trying to do fractions, and I just didn't understand fractions when I was seven.

I skipped school on a couple of occasions. My father had an office in Windsor, which was about two miles away. I remember a couple of times nipping out to see him because I loved going to his office and then he had to call the school to say I was there.

I loved sport at that school though. That was one great thing for me, playing tennis, rugby – all the sports activities.

I've never liked being mediocre. When I was playing tennis, I was competitive. If I lost points or games, I'd end up chucking my racket down. I always believed that I would get to Wimbledon and I wanted to be the world's best tennis player, and even though obviously I was nowhere near good enough to be the best in the country, let alone the world, it didn't stop me from playing whenever I could. Every spare minute of every day I was hitting a ball against the house wall or playing against the garage pretending it was Bjorn Borg at Wimbledon. My mum, in the kitchen, would just put her earplugs in. I went back into a state school and then from the age of 11, right through to 18, I played tennis seven days a week. I was seriously competitive. I played county tennis, I played regional tennis. I played all the UK competitions up and down the country.

I knew tennis was just a game but at the end of the day it's about winning and losing and the last thing I wanted to do was lose. When I missed silly shots it would make me furious. Tennis is an intelligent game – in many ways it is similar to business and the skills I learned playing tennis have helped my career as a businessman. In tennis you've got to work out the strategy, understand your playing partner, and then assess your competitor, sizing up their game. It is important to have confidence from the moment you walk onto the court. I was a good tennis player, but I was just not a very good loser. It's the same deal now. I play against Andrew Castle, a former UK number one tennis player. The last time I played him I broke his serve on the first game of the opening set. You could see him stomp round the court wondering what on earth was going on – I'd only played once or twice in the previous two years. I could see him getting upset (albeit in a friendly manner) so I relished that in the first few games and then all of a sudden he was winning game after game. Before we got to the end of the set we had to stop, because I didn't want him to win the set 6–1. And I was tired. My heart was racing twice its normal speed so I said, 'Let's play another game another time.' The next time I play Andrew Castle, I will make sure I've had about three months' training!

There is, however, a key difference between tennis and business. Business is not about winning at all costs. In business you are trying to find ways where you both benefit, rather than winner takes all – I don't want to do a deal with somebody and walk out thinking, 'Ah, got them.' That's not how my mind-set works. With a business deal I want my business colleagues to walk out of the room thinking that they are really happy, while I'm thinking exactly the same. In tennis the last thing I want to do is walk off a court while somebody else wins the match. I'm out there to win, whereas in business I want both of us to win.

However, when it comes to competitors in the market, sport and business converge. Competitive business is about winning. I want to be better than all the other competitors out there.

Tennis is a game with two facets. When you play singles, you're out on the court on your own, there's no one else to help you and no one else to blame, and it's about beating your opponent. When you play doubles, there's somebody else that you've got to rely on, work with, communicate with, and for me, that's just like building a business. As an entrepreneur you start on your own, you need to win every deal while you are building your business, making money and getting the deals away. Then you start employing staff and then the business becomes collaborative and you work as a team to plan a strategy of how to beat the competition and how to win opportunities.

My first company was a business based on building computer systems and providing computer support. It was successful during the boom time of the 1980s, but I lost sight of the key elements of running a company. I was carried away with my own success, thinking it was easy, without understanding the risks. I was supplying equipment on credit without properly evaluating the customers or making sure that they were financially secure. At some point there was going to be a problem ... and there was! Several companies that

I was supplying went bust owing tens of thousands of pounds and that ensured the collapse of my business. There was no warning. One day one of my engineers called to say the liquidators had arrived at one of the businesses that we supplied. I rushed over but it was too late – everything that we had supplied to them had been taken away and the company was bust.

People react to business collapse in different ways: for the first few days I was fire-fighting, hoping to recover the situation. I think it took me 24 hours before I realised I couldn't save the company. At 29 years of age, I lost everything. I had nowhere to live and after living with my parents for a few weeks I moved into the office building where I started from. I lived there for six months thinking about what I should do and how I could rebuild and start again. I didn't have any money or a car.

I didn't feel lonely because I've got some great friends but I'm very much an individual. I wasn't sitting around weeping. I was thinking, 'Well I've got myself into this situation, I'm going to get out of it. It's as simple as that. There's no point crying over spilt milk. I've lost my BMW, my Porsche, my house. I've lost everything. Well it's not the end of the world.' I'd put myself in that situation through naivety. I'm not naive any more.

Very few entrepreneurs have a smooth glide upwards. Venture capitalists in the USA very often say they back people who have lost a business at least once or twice because they've gained an immense amount of experience from their early mistakes. They are worth backing.

In retrospect, the main business lesson from my company collapse was that I got too carried away generating sales without looking at the financial risk to the company. If I'd taken credit insurance out on my sales ledger that company would still be alive.

In 1998 I started Phones International Group. It was clear to me that everybody was soon going to be walking around with a mobile phone. Even though at that time the mobile phone was a huge, heavy box, it seemed obvious that everybody would want to communicate on the move.

The market for phones operated via retail outlets on the high street. I'd been in computer distribution and understood how to leverage my buying power by negotiating good deals with the manufacturers, so I worked with a manufacturer and bought large volumes of products and supplied the smaller players who couldn't afford to buy in large volume. For the first year of my business I focused on supplying only Ericsson products. We knew so much about their range, and we became product champions.

I knew it would make me wealthy. I had no idea it would make me tens of millions. There were probably a thousand similar businesses starting but what we did and the way that we differentiated ourselves in the market was unique. Nobody else had entered the market and said they were going to supply just one product set and build a one-product reputation. My strategy created a good tight relationship with the manufacturer. I knew that that way we could buy bigger volumes, so we could be most competitive in the market and our business escalated. We were one of the fastest growing businesses in Europe at that time. Was I lucky? I don't think so; it was strategy, foresight and passionate drive, alongside very hard work – seven in the morning until late at night. Having a vision is one of the most important assets when starting a business. I love being creative, visualising where I am going. It makes it easier to go further when you can already see what you are trying to achieve.

In the first three or four months there were only a couple of us and then as the business really started to grow we ramped up with a small sales team; we hired a finance accountant, then a marketing team, secretarial and administration and by the end of the first 12 months I had a complete infrastructure. Recruitment of the team was not easy because we were clearly a small company. At that point we wanted to recruit locally so it was a matter of talking to a few people and looking at the local area – for example, one of the local mobile-phone retailers had one or two very good individuals working in their shop. We interviewed people within the sector who had energy and drive. Employing people with promise is a key element of my success.

Many of the people who came for interviews almost didn't get as far as the door with me. People would turn up thinking, 'I'm in a job, not sure if I feel like a change, I'll just turn up and see what it's like.' Those people lasted about three minutes with me because that sort of attitude just doesn't cut it. I'm looking for somebody who walks into the meeting room looking sharp and clean cut, and who has investigated the business they're coming into. I wanted to know 'Why should I employ you? What is it about you that's going to make a difference? What can you tell me about my own business? What can you do differently?' My advice is that you can cut out the three interviews that many large companies feel are important, and are simply 'niceties': how's your mum and dad and what's your previous career history and what do you want to do? Let's get down to the bottom line. The bottom line is, are you good enough to work for me?

I wanted to grow an international telecoms business so I wanted a name on the tin that said what it did. We had an office in France and today we have an office in Romania – we started a large operation there for our IT services. My telecoms group is now a very big internet-software developer – as well as supplying a product we do a huge amount of development work. We develop systems and integration, websites and portals to some of the world's leading companies. So, for example, we work with Vodafone, which has a great benefit for us because we not only take care of the internet and website. Margins are important to any business and we are now moving from our percentage margin business to a fulfilment model with less inventory risk and a higher margin.

I am involved in many other areas of business – PJ Investments, which looks after the *Dragons' Den* investments and other investments I make in the market, a property portfolio and Peter Jones TV, which was born out of a hit show in the USA called *American Inventor*. We've built a television media company with the view to focusing on factual entertainment programmes.

Being on television has opened my eyes to a very big opportunity within the TV media business, and my link in with telecommunications and what we do on the web, television and media over the next 20 years in my personal opinion will be web-based. I predict that more people will look at streaming and will use the internet and broadband to view television programmes on demand. The market will transform from set-top boxes where you just change the channel to integrating new systems that will be computer-based. You'll be able to look at the internet, surf the web while you are still watching television.

Convergence of the internet and television is my vision. People will be watching TV on their mobile phones. There will be video clips on your mobile phone so you'll watch segments of shows. You might be on the train and don't want to miss your favourite hour-long programme so you can watch that as well, and you will be able to view film downloads and interactive live television. You will use your phone to connect to a video conferencing system so when you travel abroad you will be able to have a full screen. I look forward to being able to connect wirelessly to the hotel screen and being able to say goodnight to my children when I have to be away from home on business.

My investment business is always looking for new projects. Since my time on *Dragons' Den* I have received a large number of proposals. My team review them and the contributing entrepreneurs get feedback on their ideas, giving them a steer on what to do. Perhaps a few will get a phone call saying we want to talk to them further.

I'm very excited about this work. We get thousands of emails every week telling us how great it is that we're here to listen to their ideas and that it's just nice to get it off their chest. It's like somebody having a secret and being unable to tell anyone. People have held business ideas in their heads for so long that they just want that tick in a box that says, 'Peter Jones thinks it's not a bad idea', or 'Peter Jones thinks it's a really cold idea and I should shelve it. Well at least I've had a go.'

One example of a new company I have invested in is wines4business.com, supplying wine directly to corporate clients. Philip Lucas (who was a friend of mine) had a tiny wine business and came to us with the concept of working directly with companies and supplying wines at a good discount for all of their events. As a corporate customer ourselves we know that when you have an event you often buy the wine locally – sometimes you even send your secretary round the corner to buy your wine from the off-licence. A company that can handle this, deliver next day, hassle-free, offers a great service. The wines4business.com system is on the web so the secretary can click on the order with their account, opening up a massive market. There is also a branded wine club that supplies to the end user directly and adds value to our clients' businesses. We own 47 per cent of that company with a very small investment of about £150,000.

wines4business.com is a differentiated service that wasn't being offered in the market at that time. It's a question of tweaking an idea, finding ways to make it really different from all the rest.

I am not interested in putting money into a business and just letting it ride. I am not a gambler; I don't throw my money around and even when I go to the races I probably only take a couple of hundred pounds with me at most. I ask myself, 'Does it grab me? Do I really want to get involved?' and finally, 'Can Peter Jones make a difference?' Because if I can't add value to a business I am involved with, what's the point?

DEBORAH MEADEN
THE MARKETEER

Deborah Meaden joined Dragons' Den *for the third series and is the only female Dragon. Born in 1959, she launched her own glass and ceramics export company soon after leaving college. She set up one of the first Stefanel fashion franchises in the UK and ran a prize bingo conces sion at Butlins before joining her family's amusement-arcade business, starting on the shop floor and working her way up to Operations Director. She moved out of amusements into Weststar Holidays which at the time owned one holiday park. She was quickly promoted to Managing Director and grew it into a business providing high-quality family holidays for over 100,000 people per year.*

In 1999 Deborah acquired the major shareholding in Weststar in a management buyout. She sold the company in a deal worth £33 million while retaining a 23 per cent stake and an active role in its running. She is always on the lookout for good investment opportuni- ties – her first was a market-research company, reflecting her own interest in marketing, brands and communications.

Deborah now lives in the Southwest of England, splitting her time between London and the home which she shares with her husband Paul, Friday the cat, two dogs, five horses, 11 chickens and four Indian Runner ducks. Deborah has always understood her customers, and she goes out of her way to find out what the customer wants whether it be a service or a product – that care and attention to detail and refusal to compromise has given her the edge.

I'm a doer. My advice is always, 'Stop thinking about it and *do* it.' I live for the moment; whatever I'm involved in right now is the most important thing I could possibly be doing. Once it's done, I don't reflect; I don't beat myself up about possible mistakes. I just focus on the next project.

My parents were always involved in the leisure industry. This was often highly seasonal which meant that we had to earn as much as we could during the summers. My parents split their summers between Longleat in Wiltshire and Butlins in Minehead. Looking back it was an odd sort of childhood where, from a very young age when my elder sister and I had proper jobs during the school holidays but it was quite normal to me and I loved it. I also learnt that to be successful you have to do whatever needs to be done … a lesson I have never forgotten. We had very little money in the early days, but I had an incredibly resourceful mother who absolutely wasn't going to let the world get her down. My mother had no time for self-pity. I'm the same – not interested. Get on and do it, because nobody else is going to do it for you. I am responsible for my own life.

I was always going to run my own business. It never entered my head that I was ever going to work for anybody. When I was seven years old I set up a flower stall at our gate, stocked with flowers I'd picked from our garden. I soon realised that the location was wrong because everybody was driving the wrong way, so I moved my stall to our neighbour's gate, much to her disgust. I remember the neighbour saying I shouldn't be allowed to do it, but my parents were quite proud of me!

An early lesson from the flower stall was that location is all-important; later, with the holiday parks, it was vital.

I'm a very confident person, and I think confidence is catching. People buy from confident people. When I left school, I wanted to be in London, but I had neither a reason nor the means to be there. So I answered an advertisement for a sales-room model in a London fashion house. You had to be 5 ft 8 and I'm 5 ft 1, but I thought, if I can just get in the door, I can talk my way into a job. And that's what happened. I must have sold my skills to the manager, because height is a hard thing to disguise and despite his first comment being, 'You're not 5 ft 8, are you?' he took me on. Clearly he believed that my confidence and sales ability – or sheer gall – would make up foor my lack of height and that I would be an asset in the showroom.

I was always looking for ways to start my own business. After business school I stayed with a friend in Italy and noticed some wonderful glass and ceramics and thought, 'Now I haven't seen this in the UK.' I had no assets and no capital, so I decided that a way of getting started would be to use my sales skills and act as an agent.

I thought, I don't have to buy a load of stock, I don't actually need money, I just need me.

I was only 19. How did I get in the door? I didn't know you couldn't. I literally just knocked on doors and said, 'Look, I've got no network, but I will work my socks off to sell your goods in the UK', and they bought it. I got the goods into Top Drawer, which is *the* most prestigious giftware exhibition. From there, I started selling to some of the bigger stores, like Harvey Nichols. I didn't make much money, but I eked out a living, had a pretty good time, and learned a huge amount.

In Italy I'd come across Stefanel – it was like Benetton, but I thought it was better. Benetton was huge in the UK at the time, so I thought, I can make Stefanel a serious UK competitor. I had experience now, but no money. I walked into the Stefanel shop in Knightsbridge and said, 'How about doing a franchise?' and I talked them into giving me one of the very first franchises, down in the Southwest, which is where I'm from. I went into partnership with a friend: he provided the premises, I secured the franchise, and it went very well. I didn't see myself as a shopkeeper all my life, so he bought me out. At last I had some money!

I went through a series of businesses after that, but the one I learned most from was a prize bingo concession at Butlins. It's a really ergonomic business. You deal directly with the customers and if your customer doesn't like you, they get up and they walk away, and you see them do it. It was a brilliant lesson in understanding that time is money – if you mess around and your games are going too slowly, it costs you money. The quality has got to be there, otherwise your customer will tell you about it.

Recognising people was the key. In a day I'd probably see a thousand people. I tried to recognise and remember most of them and if I couldn't, I learned to look as if I did. Recognise people, make them feel important, and they'll remember you – that's what I learned. Bingo is huge, and the reason people do it is social, so you've got to provide a good social environment, make people feel welcome, make them feel a part of what's going on.

It's the same with the whole of the leisure industry, whether it's holidays, arcades, fast-food outlets, even shopping – yes, shopping's a leisure activity. Why should the customer choose what you're offering over what's available next door? It's all about environment. You need to create a pleasing environment in which people feel safe.

My next step was to join the amusement-arcade business which my parents had started. Again, the emphasis was on environment and good service; there might be seven arcades on the sea front, so how did we get people to choose ours? It's all about tiny little tweaks – carpets, comfortable seats, making things easy for the customer. The maximum you could win at that time was something like £1.40, so it wasn't about winning, it was about a good ambience. What I would say to anyone wanting to start a business, is why would the customer choose *you*?

Throughout my career to date, I'd been building up a picture of how people wanted to spend their leisure time. The business my parents were in was concession-based, a model I have never been comfortable with, and when the opportunity came up to buy a holiday park which was struggling within a large organisation, we went for it. This was in 1988. We ended up with a group of holiday parks, providing high-quality family holidays for more than 100,000 people a year.

I was confident that I knew how to improve the parks and provide what people wanted. The location had to be special – I'd never buy a park in a bad location. We built facilities: in this country, weather is always going to be a problem, so we built these indoors – swimming pools, restaurants, clubs, tennis courts, adventure playgrounds. This way, we could extend the holiday season. We managed to keep one of our parks open for 48 weeks, which was a record. It sounds obvious now, but we were one of the first parks to build indoor pools.

Anyone who believes that working in a family business sounds like a cushy option is very wrong. There is a whole added dynamic and you have to be tough to face some pretty difficult issues head on if the business is going to thrive. My family have always been very clear: business is business and if you look after that it looks after you. That is a very good ethos for anyone working with close friends or family and keeps you focused on the stuff that matters and away from the personal issues.

In 1999, keen to secure my future, I did a management buyout with a plan to grow the business through acquisition and development within the existing Parks. This was a long-term plan but then I realised that while my heart was still in it, my head was telling me that the market conditions were difficult for acquisition and maybe I should look down the other end of the telescope and consider a sale.

After a hotly contested bid process I sold half my stake in the business to a private equity firm in a deal worth £33m. I still owned 23 per cent of Weststar and played an active role in acquisitions, development and sales and marketing but withdrew from the day-to-day management of the company. In 2007, just 2½ years later, I sold the remainder of my stake at which time Weststar was valued at £83 million.

With less time now spent on the day-to-day running of a business I have had more time to become involved with other investments. I like seed start-ups and I enjoy being able to really make a difference. Most of all I love success and successful people and get a real buzz out of seeing a business I am involved in flourish.

I think my greatest strengths lie in sales, marketing and customer understanding. I thought I'd better put my money where my mouth is, so I've invested in a research company. I'm a great believer in research; anyone thinking of starting a business needs to establish whether there's a market, or a need for the product. With this company, I've invested in the person, because although the market-research area is heavily populated, this guy has a unique angle on it. It's highly interactive; the minute the first survey is done, the person who has commissioned the survey can look at the results.

The internet means that researching a potential market has never been easier. The key is to make your research specific and relevant. You need to find out exactly who the current providers are in the existing market, establish their strengths and their weaknesses, and work out what they are failing to provide.

A lot of people try to over-complicate sales and marketing. It is neither difficult nor mysterious. Don't try to be too clever, just think, who is my customer, what do they want, where do I find them and how do I talk to them? It is important to have a clear image of your typical customer: for instance, when I invested in MixAlbum I asked Ian to create a typical customer including age, style, marital status, hobbies, leisure activities, music taste, what they would read, newspapers, magazines, etc ... even a name and a photograph! Although these are fictitious people, they embody the essence of the customer and serve as a constant reference for communications – would this person read this? Would they say that? It also serves as an excellent tool for all people working in the organisation or consulting for the organisation to actually put a face to the people they are dealing with.

What makes a successful entrepreneur? Confidence; an enquiring mind; a habit of constantly trying to make things better, looking for what's missing. A lot of people think that passion is enough, but it's not. Don't get too passionate too early. To succeed you need to be able to take a cool, calculated and critical look, and if you are convinced this is an opportunity worth going for *then* get passionate. This is an odd balancing act that requires a bit of steeliness, but one worth perfecting.

Planning your business step by step at an early stage, with

timescales and milestones, is an excellent idea. Your plan will help keep you on track; it can be a good motivator, because it can show you what you've already achieved, or it can be an early warning system – if, say, you're constantly failing to meet the deadlines you've set yourself, then it's time for a re-think.

Yes, research is important, but don't get bogged down in it. I set my research: I say this is what I need to know about this business, I don't need to know any more and I mustn't know any less. When you really know your stuff, then you're ready to pitch your business. Be clear about what drives your business forward. Give a concise, credible message. You need to convince your potential investor that you have a 'handle' on the important stuff that will really make your business tick.

I won't invest in a good person if they haven't got a good product. For any business to work, you have to establish a reason why people would want what you're offering. There's no point in promoting a bad product, because you'll be found out very quickly. On the other hand, you can have a fantastic product, but if you don't know how to market it properly it'll remain the best-kept secret in the world. One of my personal strengths is that I know how to get the message out to potential customers.

Being driven, ambitious and confident can also be a dangerous combination. In my rush for rapid growth I acquired two holiday parks which were frankly a mistake, and which on reflection I only bought because I wanted to grow and grow fast! The lesson here is to be brave and honest enough to recognise mistakes and deal with them quickly. Reversing a decision or action may be a very public statement of the original error but refusing to recognise and rectify it is costly both in time and money, and could ultimately lead to business disaster. Don't try to run before you can walk. Make your first business your perfect model – and recognise the things that don't work. Learn your business lessons, hone it, mould it, pull it, stretch it until you are happy with it and then roll it out!

Once you're ready to pitch to investors, rehearse in front of someone you respect and admire. Memorise key points. Use your own language – anything else will sound false. Present yourself as smart and well-groomed, but at the same time you've got to feel comfortable in what you're wearing, you've got to be yourself. Above all, be honest; all good investors have in-built bullshit detectors!

Honesty is very important to me personally. I don't suffer fools gladly. One of my faults is that I can be too blunt, but it is better to tell someone straight away that their idea won't work, rather than give them false hopes and allow them to waste valuable time and, probably, money. I'm very straightforward – bitching and grumbling are not allowed among my staff. If someone has something to say, they must say it openly. I will not tolerate cliques.

When I'm making business decisions I can be quite dispassionate. On TV, my face is deadpan and, yes, there's a coolness there. I have even been called an 'Ice Queen' but that must be by somebody who hasn't seen the laughter lines – you don't get those by being cold and humourless! I have great fun in business and great fun in the Den, but I know when to be serious and I am not afraid of telling it as it is if needs be. I've made mistakes, but I've learned from them, and I've avoided major disasters. I believe in taking risks, but not in silly gambles. What would I do if I were to lose all my money? I'd make it again, of course!

THEO PAPHITIS
THE RETAIL EXPERT

Theo Paphitis was born in Limassol, Cyprus in 1959. His family emigrated to England when Theo was six years old, and he attended the local comprehensive school in North London where they failed to detect his dyslexia, then left to take a job as a tea-boy and filing clerk at a City of London insurance brokers.

He made his first step into retail at the age of 18 as a sales assistant for Watches of Switzerland. At 20, he moved into finance and became involved in commercial mortgage sales. At 23, he set up his own company, later developing a taste for turning around failing businesses.

Theo has purchased ailing businesses such as the stationery chains Ryman and Partners and La Senza and Contessa lingerie chains, and turned them into successful and profitable companies. In the last 12 months he sold the lingerie businesses to private equity firm Lion Capital and added to the stationery business by purchasing 61 Stationery Box stores. He has several other business interests including a 50 per cent share in Red Letter Days, which he purchased with fellow Dragon, Peter Jones.

Theo lives in Surrey with his wife Debbie. He has five children, Dominic, Zoe, Alex, Hollie and Annabelle, as well as two grand children. He married young and, keen to support his wife and kids, threw himself into work, picking up priceless retail tips from the shop floor. He still puts those lessons to use as a multi-millionaire business person. Here we see how he has become the UK's best-known retail-recovery expert.

Do you ever finally 'make it' in business? I don't think so. And that's what drives me to keep going. The day I say I've 'made it' in business will be the day I die or retire. In my case, it would probably be the former.

When I started out at 16, I was working for a Lloyds' broker, surrounded by public-school chaps – not many of them had much business sense as far as I could see. I was a tea-boy. No, not even that – I was the assistant to the tea-stirrer! He was the official tea-boy, I just helped out.

I had paired up with Mrs P by then and I was finding it very difficult to settle down on the rather meagre salary I was earning. To be honest with you I didn't know what I wanted at that age but I saw this job advertised in the *Evening Standard* working for Watches of Switzerland. It paid more than I was earning, substantially more. I went for the interview and it was so unlike the City. There, I would have an interview and be told they would write to me. Weeks later, the 'Dear John' letter would come floating through the door. At Watches of Switzerland, I went for the interview and, shock, horror, I was offered the job on the spot. That was my first experience of the dynamics of the retail industry.

I enjoyed retail from the start. I was in one of those stores where the door was locked permanently and people had to ring the buzzer and be let in. You never knew who was going to come through that door, a bit like the staircase in the Dragons' Den. There was a genuine excitement about not knowing what would happen next. When a customer came in you were on your mettle right away: you took an interest in them, you started analysing what that person actually wanted, you got really involved. The whole business including, naturally, closing the sale was right up my street.

What I want to emphasise here is this. The great thing about retail is that at an incredibly low level you experience marketing, you experience sales, you experience customer service, you experience design. Those are wonderful things to know about at whatever level you are in retail and you can learn them right off the starting block.

I stayed at Watches of Switzerland until I was 20. By then, I needed more money again. As a salesman in a prestige watch store you can only earn so much – I was a pretty good salesman but I was reaching the maximum on my earning ability even if I became the branch manager. It was never going to give me enough money and big money was my ambition. So I moved back to the finance industry, and you know what? I found I could use a lot of the skills I now had – the salesman skills, the marketing skills, all honed in the few years I had been in retail. Of course I have always believed this and still preach that business is very much about common sense. The lack of common sense out there never fails to surprise me. Without having any formal training in reading accounts or running businesses I was meeting people in business, working on the finance side, raising finance for the company. It astonished me how many of the people I was talking to were totally unimpressive when it came to doing the things they needed to do to put their businesses right.

I wonder now how I must have appeared – some kid, turning up at clients at this very tender young age. Fortunately for me, I always looked a bit older than I was: slightly thinning on top, careful never to tell people my actual years. And I would look at their businesses. I was good at identifying the issues they had and giving them advice. Once again, I was using those skills I got from my first job in retail. What is wonderful for me is how I've been able to link my two careers and my two loves: retail and turning round businesses.

Well, I'm one of those people who have the concentration span of a gnat and three years later, I made the decision. I would go it alone. That's either in you or it's not. Some people are comfortable in an environment where decisions are made for them, some of us are a bit less structured. We like to take control of our own destiny. So there I was, 23 years old and running my own company. And it worked out. I made some money in the commercial property boom of the 1980s and kept going from there, always looking for the right deal, the right opportunity. I learned focus, hard work and, most of all, to identify and know my market.

The most important rule for me has always been to choose the right target. However tempting they may seem, some companies can never be turned round. You can spend your whole life and oceans of capital and you will still end up no more than a busy fool. You have lavished every waking hour on this company and what's the result? A business with nowhere to go. Choosing the correct target – that is the key to giving yourself a fighting chance. I only look at businesses that are struggling. If a business is flying it is no good to me. I want a business that has got potential, that needs my input, my care, my attention, my detail and my passion, for example Movie Media Sports.

Now, Movie Media Sports was a sports-marketing agency in which I invested 40 grand for 50 per cent. I had it for about 10 years and made around £6 million from it. Mind you, I have to admit, that investment was all about having fun. I like sport and it was great to be around all the sports grounds, have passes to go to all the events and make money out of it at the same time. It doesn't get better than that, does it?

But essentially, I am always drawn to brand. A business that people recognise. Yes, it may have lost its shine, it may even look like it's on its last legs, but brand can still give you a substantial edge when you come to relaunch. I prefer the simple approach. 'Keep It Simple, Stupid' has always been my motto and, for me, it has to be a brand, it has to be niche and it usually needs to be in trouble.

Ryman ticked all those boxes. It had been around a long time, it was a household name, the only specialist commercial stationery retailer in the high street. But when I bought it in 1995, it was in a terrible state. It had actually lost about £8–10 million the year before it went into receivership. Staff were demoralised, the stores were stark, there was no stock. We were entering the computer age when everybody was telling me that paper and writing instruments was a thing of the past. It was a 'sunset' industry as opposed to a 'sunrise' industry – that was the buzz word in those days. Basically it was an old dog. But I love the old dogs if everybody recognises them! I had known Ryman as a kid, I actually shopped there. I just needed to plan properly and address its glaring problems. So here is what I did.

First and foremost, I had to bring everyone on side. I needed to get them buying into my dream, my ambitions for the company and the brand before I did anything else. If I couldn't do that I knew I would never succeed. At head office, I had to ensure people were actually doing jobs that were necessary rather than jobs for the job's sake. But the big challenge was to re-energise and re-motivate the people who worked in the stores.

How did I do it? I did what I have done in all my businesses. I made sure the store staff had direct access to me. I would go to the stores, work with them and listen to them. I hear people endlessly talk about 'communications processes' and 'leadership skills', but the key to Ryman in that first year was the constant dialogue I had with the store staff. I reckon in the vast majority of failed businesses you will find that is one of the biggest issues – staff feel separated from the boss, they cannot have a direct dialogue. I say a hands-on approach cannot be overestimated. You have to keep your finger on the pulse to know whether the business is healthy or dying.

It was also important for me to see where we could increase sales and where we could cut costs. At that time, the recession of the late 1980s and early 1990s was well and truly in play. I knew the previous management had left us over-rented in property, so I renegotiated all the leases. Some landlords were helpful, some told me to get on my bike – in which case, I sent the big lorries round, emptied the store and gave them the keys back. No point being somewhere if you can't make a living – you're back to being the busy fool.

Finally, I had to gain the confidence of the suppliers, restock the business and make sure that we provided the service that our customers needed. And then, hey presto, the results started coming through. I had been right. The old dog – the brand – was hugely strong. It had very loyal followers. As long as we gave them the service they wanted and had the product in the stores at the right time, customers came in.

For the staff too, a sense that they could share in the success of the business made a whole heap of difference. All my staff are given incentives – from the warehouse to the drivers, the store staff to the post lady. Everyone single one of them. They know their success or lack of it is going to have a direct impact on their earnings. As well as financial incentives I like to motivate the staff through our conferences and social functions. At our conferences, following a fun and exciting way of delivery of some key messages and information during the day, we spend the evening having dinner followed by drinks at the bar. I have found these occasions useful for getting lots of feedback on what's going on in the stores and the business. There is also the fun we have every year when me and other senior members of my team join our store managers on a company 'outing'. Last May 150 of us spent a week at an all-inclusive resort in Mauritius and in previous years we have been to St Lucia, Barbados and other similarly exotic places. Once again a chance to celebrate success, as well as an opportunity to spend quality time with my team and meet staff running the stores. When I bought Ryman they held their conferences in a basement below one of the stores using an overhead projector and followed by cheese sandwiches.

And the funny thing is that, once again, this all comes from what I learned back in those early days at Watches of Switzerland. I learned that Head Office never listened, so I do listen. I learned there was a 'them and us', so I spend serious time in my stores with my staff. I learned as a young salesman that if I sold a product that had a yellow sticker on it I got 10 per cent commission instead of a-couple-of per cent. Surprise, surprise – guess what most of my sales were? So now I make sure I always give proper incentive to my staff. Once I understood how people tick even better than how a watch ticks, those early experiences were easy to translate and trans-fer to all my own retail businesses.

Let me give you another example. La Senza, the lingerie chain I used to own. Same story. I got under the skin of the business and made sure the staff believed in the brand. I gave them incentives and together we attended to all the basic stuff. Retail is all about detail, about being sure that everything is right for the customer. At La Senza I took a pride in making our customers feel special. They might only have been coming in to purchase a multi-buy of briefs or a bra-and-panty set that cost less than £15, but we would make them feel great about themselves. Their purchase would get wrapped in tissue paper, they got scented beads in the bag.

Compare that with the experience at the supermarket. You are rushing round with the trolley, you find the garment you want – perfectly decent – you chuck it in with the milk and the frozen pizza. You pull it out of the bag when you get home and it drops on the kitchen floor with the toothpaste and yoghurt. It probably hangs about on the stairs for a while before it gets to your bedroom. How do you think you feel about that garment when you put it on? At La Senza, we could have slashed millions off our costs every year but, trust me, we wouldn't have had a business. What I was interested in was product, and customer service. Surely, you will say, that's just common sense? You are right – 90 per cent of business is all about common sense. But amazingly, common sense is not common. If it was common everyone would have it and everyone would be able to do what I do. Then how would I make a living?

I have to tell you, it is highly unlikely that anyone will be successful in a business if they don't have the passion for it. It has always helped me that I am doing what I enjoy. It makes me stronger and more determined to: 1) make money, 2) have fun, 3) not forget to make more money. The one thing I wish is that I had shown more confidence. People tell me I seem a supremely confident person, but I would say I am too conservative. I target high-risk situations so I come over as buccaneering, but in reality I'm just a person who does his homework. Homework, homework and yet more homework. Nothing short-term. I plan everything and get it crystal clear in my mind.

On a personal note, I have really been helped by my family life. I have been married for 30 years, I've got five children from late twenties to not-yet-teens and a couple of grandchildren besides. We married when I was eighteen and it's been the bedrock of my life. Mrs P rules the roost and the minute my driver drops me off at home and I cross that threshold, I am no longer the boss who gets pampered with all the attendant privileges. No, the gloves are off and I get ordered about and have chores like everyone else and slot in as part of the team! Yes, having a stable family background is great. You have a nightmare day and finally you say 'enough' and hurry back home. Of course, when you get there the kids are screaming at you and you want to go back to work. That's also a great motivator!

Looking back over my business life so far, the biggest mistake I ever made when I was younger was believing that professionals – such as accountants or solicitors – are always right. I learned very quickly that is actually a load of old tosh. Now, whenever I buy a business, I ask myself, what is going to happen to my money if I invest? That means getting under the surface of every part of that business, understanding the dynamics of the business as a whole. I consider what happens if things go wrong. What is my plan B, my plan C? Should I combine elements of these into yet another plan? Never fall into the trap of ignoring the facts. There is no shame in walking away from a project when your analysis and market research tell you you must.

But, as I learned when I first started out, each new customer, each situation properly studied and understood is a new beginning. Hold on to your excitement about not knowing what will happen when the next one comes through the door.

Now I'm in the Den, people send me ideas all the time. There is one on my desk as I am writing. It came in this morning and, to be honest, it's barking mad! But I look at them all. That's what you do if you're really in business. You keep your eyes open, you do your homework, you check it out from every angle. You think about your staff and your customers.

And then? Just use your common sense.

DUNCAN BANNATYNE
THE SERIAL ENTREPRENEUR

Duncan Bannatyne grew up in Clydebank and joined the Navy as a teenager. After spending his twenties moving from one job to another, Duncan's business career began with an ice-cream van purchased for £450. He soon expanded and bought more vans and eventually sold the business and set up a chain of nursing-homes. He sold his nursing-home business Quality Care Homes for £46 million in 1996 and his children's nursery chain Just Learning for £22 million. He has since expanded into health clubs, hotels and house building. He recently aquired 24 health clubs from the Hilton Hotel Company and rebranded them as Bannatyne health clubs. Duncan was awarded an OBE for services to business and charity and was recently made an honorary Doctor of Science by Glasgow Caledonian University. He was also made an Honorary Fellow of UNICEF for his services to charity in 2003. Duncan has also helped fund two orphanages in Romania and Colombia working with the charity Scottish International Relief.

Duncan was Awarded Master and Overall Entrepreneur of the Year in 2003 and ranked 9th in a table of the UK's top 100 entrepreneurs by respected business journal, Management Today, *in 2005. Duncan is a people person and his story of success demonstrates the importance of knowing and trusting your team.*

The single most important factor in any company is the people who work for it. Arguably, they are even more important than the product itself as, undoubtedly, employees can hold the critical difference between success and failure in their hands. Effectively utilising human resources and hiring the correct people for the correct positions is crucial to the prosperity of any company.

One of the reasons I maintain that every person has it within themselves to become a successful businessman or woman is because I am something of an accidental entrepreneur myself. Almost all of my businesses possessed an element of chance at the inception of the idea and it was only after studying the field that I realised what an excellent opportunity each notion represented. Right at the start of my career, for example, I was selling cars at auction when I spied an ancient ice-cream van slowly trundling into the lot. Immediately, even impulsively, I decided to begin selling ice cream. Within a short space of time and with a lot of graft I had acquired a fleet of vans and had begun to turn a healthy profit. All this ran contrary to the fact that when I started Duncan's Super Ices I had nothing – no business experience, no degree, no assets, no capital and no influential contacts – but I learned quickly.

Each day I resolved to study the performance of my fleet. I would tally the stock on every van from the start and from the end of the day and compute the profit margin for each vehicle All my drivers worked on commission only, which encouraged harder work than perhaps a standard wage might have done. This was an early prototype of a formula I have used throughout my business life – attempting to identify and implement employee contracts and deals that are beneficial to everyone. In this case, an employee would be rewarded with better money for more industry, while I would never find myself overpaying a driver with a propensity for indolence.

My daily accounting yielded valuable results. First and obviously, the calculations pinpointed the best drivers on my fleet. Second, they also allowed me to understand some peculiar anomalies. For example, I found that some of my best drivers were being held back by their families – their wives did not want them out working past 9 pm, which was when some of the best money could be made. In retrospect, even at this early stage of my business career, I was learning to understand what type of person I would be looking for to fill particular positions in my companies and to take into consideration nuances such as family life and how that might affect a person's outlook.

I had to learn some pragmatism, too. I recall one occasion when I had two people working one of the ice-cream vans. They always turned a decent profit for me, but I could deduce from my calculations that they were stealing £50 from the till each week. I confronted them about the issue and eventually they ended up leaving the company. Unfortunately, their replacement turned out to be a poor worker and stole even more money than they had, to the extent that this previously very profitable van began making a loss. I learned that sometimes you must look at the percentages and make sure that you are getting your fair return from the effort that's being put in by the people – whether or not they're getting a little bit more than they're entitled to is another matter.

Some entrepreneurs enjoy the security of being hands-on at all times but that goes contrary to my own belief that delegation is one of the keystones of my success. Even in those early days with the ice-cream vans I was learning about delegation. I had to – it wasn't physically possible for me to operate more than one van at once and in addition to that, as soon as the time was right, I made sure I gave myself Saturdays off!

After I sold the ice-cream business I set up Quality Care Homes for the elderly and began to expand and refine the principles I had put in place with Duncan's Super Ices. I found that many of the nurses were incredibly diligent and enthusiastic. They were passionate at ensuring that the residents were constantly active, always involved in activities and events. I wanted to grant these exceptional employees the leeway to develop their careers and their skills and to reward them with promotion and greater responsibilities. I observed how they reacted to these changes and if they grew with the job, if they handled the added pressures and were happy to take the reins, then I would reward them further. I discovered that it was all about variety – different kinds of people were able to thrive in my companies and in turn help me to make the business a success. Naturally, as with any business, some failed to seize the opportunity, but that did not stop me encouraging my brightest, most ambitious employees.

The coincidence of the ice-cream van trundling into the lot seems to have repeated itself throughout my career. For example, it was because of a skiing accident that I established Bannatyne Health Clubs. My injured leg needed strengthening, but my nearest gym was a 25-minute drive away. As I rebuilt the muscle I began to calculate the figures and became determined to build a health club of my own to service the people in my area. We now have more than 60 throughout the UK. I set up Just Learning, a chain of day-care centres, because I needed a nursery for my kids in Darlington but all the centres had waiting lists – clearly there was a demand that needed to be met. So I built my own. These businesses, along with the care homes, were all quite different and aimed at varying age groups, but crucially they all offered a valuable service to the local community and I was able to reuse my basic principles about human resources and staff development as I graduated from one business to the next.

At Quality Care Homes I discovered it was easy to attract staff who wanted a change from their job and were enthusiastic in seeking a new challenge. This was a trend that continued with the day-care centres and the fitness clubs. However, whenever a business is expanding quickly there is always a danger that recruitment is happening too fast, which often results in the hiring of inferior or ill-suited staff. Although it is important to guard against this, it is sometimes an almost necessary consequence of rapid expansion.

Concurrently, the initial boom in quality applicants dissipated as each venture grew. For example, as Bannatyne's Health Clubs expanded it quickly became clear that top-class, motivated and qualified managers and gym instructors were at a premium, particularly when taking into account the growing number of other branded health clubs. This drift was echoed in our Just Learning centres where qualified staff became increasingly difficult to come by.

One way of attracting the better-quality employees would have been to simply offer higher wages than our competitors. Yet I always search for staff who believe in what we are trying to achieve, not people who are just joining for a few extra pounds in their wage packet, so we introduced training within our organisations. At Just Learning we spurred employees to gain their National Vocational Qualifications while working with us. At Bannatyne's Health Clubs we allow and encourage all our staff at all levels to undertake training that can lead to promotion, greater responsibility and, of course, a better wage. Once again, it is a policy that is mutually beneficial. Rewarding honest, hard-working, talented and ambitious staff helps to maintain consistency which is vital to children and their parents at the day-care centres and always appreciated by gym members. It also goes a long way to ensuring that morale remains high and standards are sustained. The return for me is that I know I have reliable staff and, it goes without saying, the company saves on recruitment costs.

Meanwhile, at the highest level of my business I prefer to take a more active role in recruitment procedures. All the people on my existing Board of Directors have graduated through the ranks of the business and have been working with me for long periods. My Managing Director started as my Finance Controller and my Projects Director started with me as a surveyor. They have developed me and developed my strategies and my ideas in business too. They have enjoyed their jobs and I know I can trust them to continue doing what it is I want them to do.

It is a successful arrangement and I believe it works because I know who these people are. I'm not one for team-building exercises and I do not need to play golf with staff to get to know them better. I understand them through working with them and listening to them and learning from them. It is relatively easy to appoint a high-flying finance director who enjoys two- and three-hour lunches with accountants and bank managers every day, but that is not what I am looking for. I always recall that I taught myself good business practice and developed my own acumen as I gathered experience. I discovered early on that I did not need a powerful network of contacts to be successful – my own drive and determination was far more important. Consequently the people on my board are not the types to take extended lunches or run up enormous expenses claims. I know they do not work like that because I can see how they work, how they count the pennies, how they perform their checks, how they keep an eye on the business and how they want to develop it.

In 1992 I made the decision to float Quality Care Homes on the Stock Exchange, meaning I had to appoint a number of non-executive directors to the company. In truth, I do not have much respect for non-executive directors in public companies and I found this arrangement difficult to deal with. I did not appreciate the sensation of not having complete control of my company, especially as I was allowing people I did not know properly to take a hand in the decision-making. But there are always lessons and exceptions and it was at this time that I met Michael Fallon, the Parliamentary Under Secretary for Schools who had been MP for Darlington between 1983 and 1992. He really excelled in his role on the board. Later on, when I was considering starting the nursery in Darlington, it was Michael who also saw the potential and wanted to be part of the idea. He took 10 per cent of the company and I basically handed him the reins because I knew I could trust him. He completed the forms for registration and ran the company himself. Within five years we had more than 20 centres, which was phenomenal expansion, and I sold the company for £22 million. Again, this is an example of allowing someone else to get on with doing what they are good at while I was able to stand back and survey the bigger picture.

In my company we do not have what might be termed a 'corporate culture' and I like to think that everyone has the opportunity to blossom within the business. But when it comes to recruiting for the more high-powered positions, I have grown stronger in my belief that I want to spend more time with someone before I make the final decision. When I am deciding on these top positions I am looking for skilled people who will bring knowledge and vitality to the company. Many of these types could be successful entrepreneurs in their own right, but while they have the ambition to be in the top jobs they do not relish the risks or the loneliness that running your own business entails – and believe me, if your business goes under you really are on your own. Everyone else has to look after their own families in that situation.

Consequently, a lot of people are safe and content in their top management jobs. The key is to find them and insert them into my business and make them extremely happy and satisfied. Rewards are vitally important in this regard and a few people who have worked with me have become millionaires through share options. Offering share options is a fantastic leveller and it allows people within the company to make a lot of money and to feel the benefit of their own work and talent. Similarly with my health clubs, there are always targets for the staff to hit at every single gym and generous bonuses on offer. Once more, as with the commission on the ice-cream vans and the training at all of my service businesses, everyone benefits from the efforts of everybody else. More money, more responsibility and more satisfaction for the employees and more growth, success and profit for the company as a whole.

Employing the right people is an inexact science. I think I have some instincts when it comes to hiring staff but most of the time my knowledge of someone will grow as I work with them. Circumstances can change, too. I've had managers in the past who have performed admirably in their duties for extended periods of time, only for a change in their personal life to alter their entire working outlook and output.

The instincts I believe I have gained over the years have resulted from knowing, living with, meeting and working with a broad spectrum of people. I've met people who have literally lived in sewers and I've sat on a board with high-powered, highly educated personalities. This depth of experience has allowed me to develop a sense of the sort of people I enjoy doing business with.

I like to work with people whom I can empower by giving them freedom to manage effectively. I do not necessarily look for qualifications or mountains of experience. I study the personality and, perhaps above all, I value loyalty. By delegating to trustworthy employees I am able to take a step back from the frenzy of the day-to-day business and examine the balance sheets, study the bottom line. For example, whether you have 20 health clubs or 60, one of them has to be performing the least well. Because I trust my regional managers and the managers of each club to run the business, I am free to scrutinise that underperforming club, discover why the profit margin is lower than the rest and then recommend the necessary improvements. Lastly, and crucially for me, though, the art of effective delegation allows me much more time to enjoy the most important part of my life, my family, and to take plenty of relaxing holidays in the sun!

JAMES CAAN
THE PEOPLE'S INVESTOR

The newest recruit to Dragons' Den *is James Caan, founder and CEO of the private equity firm Hamilton Bradshaw. James sees the programme as a natural extension of his key business strategy, which has always been to identify individuals who have a compelling business proposition, a credible plan, and the necessary drive, passion and integrity to succeed.*

Born in 1960, James Caan launched himself into the world of business at the age of 24 when he created the Alexander Mann Group (AMG). AMG filled a gap in the British recruitment sector by introducing executive search into the field of middle management, and from its origins as a one-man operation, Alexander Mann swiftly became one of the UK's top recruitment organisations.

Having spent 17 years developing Alexander Mann, James attracted an excellent management team headed by Jonathan Wright to take the group over and sold the company in two stages. In 2002 James decided to take a year out and followed an Advanced Management Programme at Harvard University.

Alexander Mann Group has continued to flourish. Since it sale, James has invested in numerous business ventures. He established Hamilton Bradshaw early in 2004 investing in sectors spanning from retail and property to finance, health clubs and technology. The Hamilton Bradshaw team possesses a range of expertise in a number of critical fields and James himself heads the business management side as Chief Executive.

In 2001, James won the 'Enterprise of the Year Award' sponsored by BT, for outstanding success in business. In 2003, James was named as PricewaterhouseCooper's Entrepreneur and in the same year he won the Entrepreneur category in the Asian Jewel Awards. In 2005, he was included in the list of Britain's 100 most influential and inspiring Asian people in the Asian Power 100. He has spoken at Oxford University's Said Business School, and he has recently been the Resident Entrepreneur Mentor for MBA students at the London Business School.

I knew I was going to be a businessman from a very early age. My father ran a successful textile business, and given the traditional Asian mentality that the sons will eventually take over, I naturally thought my career would be in business. However, having seen my father work seven days a week, eight hours a day, and with very little time to enjoy life, I realised that I needed to find something that both interested and excited me, while at the same time allowing me to have a good quality of life.

I grew up with my three brothers and three sisters. At an early age, I decided that school was no longer for me. I was not interested in academia, and at that stage I did not believe it to be a basic ingredient needed in order to succeed. In my teens, I joined a small specialist recruitment agency as a trainee interviewer. I earned £32 a week, plus £5 for every job I managed to fill.

With telephone sales, you have to be able to cope with rejection. You also have to develop your own style, your own personality and your confidence. I quickly grasped the hang of this; it soon became second nature to me.

Up until my early twenties I worked for three recruitment agencies, each specialising in a different sector. I did this deliberately, to get exposed to different markets. After three years, one of my clients, a financial-services company taking on investment brokers, was recruiting for sales people. I had a lot of success with this client, having placed many candidates with him. The sales director was really impressed with the way I'd understood their requirements; he took me out to lunch and offered me a job as recruitment manager of his company.

I met my Aisha, my wife, at this company when she came for an interview. She had graduated from the London College of Fashion and was one of the lucky students to be poached by a design house. Having worked there for a few months, she decided she wanted to set up her own business; her father was keen for her to do so, and her ambition was to run a boutique called House of Aisha. While she was shop hunting, she decided to look for a job to see her through that period, which is when I interviewed her. I was attracted to her immediately, so I asked her out. She told me about her business plans. I was interested in backing her, but the crazy thing was that I didn't actually have any money to back her with. I went to a shopping centre in North London where Aisha had seen a vacant shop to let; we met the manager, who told Aisha he was really inspired by her concept and that she needed to submit a credible business plan to get a shop in the centre. I pretended to be overjoyed, and I congratulated Aisha on her success, but I was secretly panicking – where was I going to find the investment which I had promised her?

She needed £30,000. I couldn't ask my father for a loan because he'd tell me I was thinking with my heart, not with my head, so I approached various banks, but they just showed me the door. Then I read a leaflet that told me that if you had a Gold Card with Lloyds then you could get a £10,000 overdraft facility. So I applied for that, successfully, and then I did the same thing with NatWest and Barclays. I got three Gold Cards and £30,000 worth of unsecured credit.

So we set Aisha up in the shop and it did really well. Of course I had to tell her where money came from and she was horrified. She was shocked that I had promised to back her without the means to do so. I apologised, but at the same time, I explained that deep down I had been confident in her drive, and that I would manage it somehow. Where there's a will, there's a way. And I must have convinced her because within a month of the shop opening, I asked her to marry me, and she accepted.

I was 24 when I launched my first company, Alexander Mann. The name was my own invention; indeed, I did everything myself.

The concept of Alexander Mann was to bring executive search to the mid-range market – until then, headhunters had only been interested in main board positions, but I thought, why not head hunt middle management as well? After all, they're the guys who make or break a company. I picked up business very, very quickly. It wasn't long before I was wondering whether this would work globally. I launched a business called Humana International with my business partner Doug Bougie, and soon we had 147 offices in 30 countries.

Alexander Mann was a great success because I identified a gap in the market, took a simple idea and then really promoted and developed that concept. Between 1985 and 1992, when I was building up the company, my understanding of how people worked and what made them tick developed enormously. I'd say my own success is based on my ability to identify the qualities within an individual that make them successful.

Having placed hundreds of people in jobs and developed lot of insight into what works and what doesn't work, I now had the capital to back those individuals. In 1992, I was joined by Jonathan Wright in running Alexander Mann, and I decided that I would start approximately one new business each year; the concept was similar to Dragons' Den. I would find somebody who had a good idea for a business and then I would put up the capital, develop the business and monitor it for 12 months.

I've always enjoyed doing something creative with my money. Just piling up cash for the sake if it is not great achievement – it's what you do with the cash that actually makes you successful. I've never been a great saver. When I was young, if I was doing well, I'd want to buy a new suit, or a car, or take a holiday. Spending money would give me the motivation to do it all again.

The best thing is to use cash to make things happen. Take my brothers and sisters, for instance – rather than just give them presents, I've helped them to go into business for themselves. Rather than feed somebody, teach them how to fish so they can learn to feed themselves for a lifetime. With my siblings, I've tried to understand it is that each one of them enjoys or what it is that they can do very well. One weekend I went to the house of one of my sisters and she gave me some samosas. Now I have grown up on samosas, but these were just amazing! So I suggested that she make some and sell them. 'What have you got to lose?' I asked her. So that Sunday, she made 250 samosas and by noon on Monday she had sold them all. Less than a month later she told me that she was making 1,000 and that all were sold as soon as they were ready. Seeing the potential, I put up the money to enable her to develop the business, with a unit and the correct machinery. Now, the business is called Nisa, and she makes 50,000 samosas a week which are then delivered across the UK. It just can't meet demand! It's phenomenal!

Another sister trained as a beautician so I set her up in a beauty salon. One brother does alterations for Jaeger, Marks and Spencer, Hugo Boss and Calvin Klein. I encouraged and motivated my brother to run that business called Altered States, which he now does very successfully. Another brother joined me running my recruitment business and now he's set up his own business in Lahore supplying researchers to the recruitment business in the UK so it's a classic off-shore model.

It's been a privilege to be a parent. My daughters are both at university, reading politics and economics respectively. They're two very bright and intelligent girls who know their own minds and are set on pursuing careers in PR/marketing and investment banking. My daughters have a much more privileged upbringing than I had, which in some ways makes it harder to motivate them. Parenting has taught me a lot about the human psyche. You could say that I've applied this knowledge to developing business, or indeed vice versa.

I've learnt that if I want my child to do something, I need to make her feel that it was her idea. For me, this is the same when you are building a business. You have to put yourself in the other person's position. I call this a win-win scenario, where both sides feel that they are gaining from the association. The people I've backed in business have generally never run a business before so I have to give a lot of support but equally I have to bring out the best in them; it's a marriage of passion and commercialism.

Building companies is like watching a child grow. When I handed over the keys to Alexander Mann Group it was a very emotional moment for me. I'd started it from nothing and at the time of handover, it was turning over about £130 million a year in sales. But it does not matter however big or successful you are, you are never secure. Every year you wonder whether you can replicate the success of the year before. I see people more talented than myself, people with bigger businesses, whose businesses collapse and they go under. Nothing lasts forever and therefore you have to treat each day as if it was your first. The minute you think you have arrived, that's when you start going backwards.

My biggest hiccup was in 1991 when the recession began to bite. We made a grand total of £1,500 profit for the entire year. I began asking myself, am I in the right business, am I wasting my time? I was really close to throwing in the towel, but then I thought, as risky as this business may be, at least it is a risk I understand. From 1992 to 1995, there was a gradual pick-up and then in 1995, the technical bubble started. I decided to take a big leap forward. We had 25 people working for us at the time. I bought a building and called it Alexander House; it had the capacity for 120. Somehow I assumed I could grow by another 100 people. If I was right, I would be a winner, if I was wrong, I would probably go bust. I decided to take the risk! And well, those were bonanza years-the work flooded in and my gamble paid off handsomely. I think that's what makes an entrepreneur; it's he who dares, wins.

RICHARD FARLEIGH
THE BUSINESS ANGEL

Richard's story is a classic rags-to-riches adventure – from the outback of Australia to the glamour of Monte Carlo. Richard studied economics and mathematics before managing a derivatives desk, a proprietary trading desk and a hedge fund in the 1980s and early 1990s. His focus at that time was on predicting big-picture trends and the effects on the currency and interest-rate markets. In the mid-1990s he semi-retired and has since operated as a 'business angel' backing exciting early-stage companies, mostly in the United Kingdom. Richard was successful because he has worked incredibly hard to understand numbers and is able to predict change. He also has a helicopter vision – his mind hovers above everyone else and he can see the bigger picture. It is his overview of the potential of new ideas that makes him an outstanding investor in new businesses. He has now left the Den but his investments continue to grow.

It could be argued that had I remained on the natural course in which my early business career took me, and hedge funds and stayed involved with the lucrative area of investment banking, I would probably be a billionaire by now. However with the success I achieved in my 20s and early 30s I came to virtually stumble upon the realisation that what I really enjoyed was investing in small businesses and working with people who possess original, exciting ideas and great drive and enthusiasm. I love the satisfaction of helping these ideas become reality and watching good small businesses achieve their full potential.

Unlike someone like Deborah Meaden, who from a young age was showing signs of entrepreneurial skill, there is nothing in my own background to suggest that I would end up being a risk-taker or successful businessman. I grew up in Australia and in my very early years I lived a fairly transient existence. I was one of 11 children and until I was three we led a difficult life, travelling the country and living in tents as my father searched for work as a sheep-shearer and an opal miner. Unfortunately my father was an alcoholic and was violent towards all of us. Consequently, at the age of just three I was placed in a foster home in Sydney.

Although still very young, it was naturally a traumatic change in the course of my life. On starting school I was not viewed as a particularly good pupil – by myself or by my teachers. In fact I was assessed as 'backward' and placed in the lowest class for 2 or 3 years before I began to exhibit a flair for mathematics. I eventually performed well at school, but was not sure how to support myself financially at university. My foster mother, had confidence in my abilities and she decided to put me forward for an aptitude exam. Surprisingly, I fared very well and once again my life was thrown onto a startlingly different path. The marks were impressive enough for the Central Bank, the Reserve Bank of Australia, to grant me one of the most generous scholarships available in the country. It was a fantastic turn of events, and it is clear to me now that I owe a debt of gratitude to my foster mum.

Having said that, even now I am convinced that the main reason she put me forward for that exam was because she was worried that I wanted to become a professional chess player. Although I wasn't a nerd I was fascinated by chess and had even been offered private sponsorship to go to London to play in tournaments. Fortunately, I realised that I would have a much more comfortable life as an economist – even a lousy one – than as a pretty good chess player, so I gave up on the idea. I still play for fun though. My party trick is playing two games of chess simultaneously while blindfolded and usually winning. I actually demonstrated this trick to my then future wife and a friend of hers when I was in South Africa. She tells me now that she was completely blown away by this ability and it was something that really attracted her to me. So, thankfully, while my chess ambitions were never quite reached, at least my obsession with the game still managed to have a wonderful effect on my private life!

University is seen by many as a chance to relax before entering the real world. That could not have been further from the truth for me. I have never worked so hard in my life as I did in those days because the scholarship meant that I worked part-time for the first 2 years of my 5 year degree. I would finish work for the central bank at around 5 pm and then attend university before catching a train home. I did not even live close to the university either, so I rarely returned before 11 pm, just leaving enough time for a little sleep before rising again at 6 am the next day to repeat the process. It was exhausting and I really hated it. Even at weekends I was busy with homework, so there was barely any respite. In the end it was worth it and I achieved first class honours of a double major in economics and maths. During my studies I had not been happy working for the bank though and found it incredibly frustrating. We were hired because we were bright, but the work they gave me was intensely mundane and I was not very good at it simply because I found it so boring. All day and every day I found myself checking boxes and studying forms and ensuring people had filled them in correctly. It was not my style and I could not believe that so many of my colleagues seemed perfectly happy to carry out these dull tasks. I remember thinking that there must be something more interesting out there.

Fortunately, I was eventually offered another scholarship, this time to study for a PhD in economics at Princeton in America. I was absolutely thrilled that such an opportunity could be presented to me – the chance to study at such a universally respected institution was flattering and very exciting. However after a lot of thought I turned it down. I just could not face the idea of spending the rest of my life trying to figure out if some numbers and equations were bigger or smaller than other numbers and equations. I was looking for something with more excitement and, sure enough, I was about to experience it. By this point it was the early 1980s and thanks to deregulation and increased competition between banks, investment banking was beginning to explode. I was told that this was an area where I could earn a lot of money, but the downside was that there was a significant risk of burn-out. That was fine by me. I decided to go and earn some money. I could worry about burning out later! At the age of 23 I left the academic world behind me and moved into the exhilarating environment of investment banking.

Taking a new career path was a huge risk in many ways because the Central Bank pretty much offered a job for life and that was what most people there accepted. You might not earn millions of dollars, but it was a safe, respected, white-collar job. At my new employers, Bankers Trust, things were more cut-throat. It was a place where you had to make money – or help others make money. It was an extremely competitive world with new products, new people and more money always entering a business that was evolving incredibly quickly. They simply could not afford to carry someone who was not paying for themselves, so if you did not make the grade you were out. It was a precarious situation. In retrospect, perhaps this was the first time that I started to feel confident about my own abilities. Despite my academic success, I had never really shaken off the feeling that I was backward in some way.

I took a pay cut to work at Bankers Trust but it was very exciting and I was very lucky to end up at such a forward-thinking company. Although not the largest, Bankers Trust was certainly the most successful investment bank in Australia at that time. It was a tremendous environment and I had so much respect for the incredible people I was allowed to work with. In contrast to some of the staid, even snobbish environments I had experienced previously, it did not matter what Sydney suburb you came from or whether you were a foster child or how old you were – if you were good at your job then there was no limit to the opportunity on offer, and I was extremely grateful for the chance to prove myself on a level playing field. Due to my mathematics background, I began by designing complicated derivatives and I figured out how to offer superior products and better prices than the big Australian banks. This was a successful activity and fairly safe because we could reduce our risk and lock-in a profit by buying in one market while covering it in another. I was still some distance away from the risk-taking I took up later. It was a thrilling time and I loved it because I relished the chance to be involved in deals worth hundreds of millions of dollars and be part of this young, booming area of business.

Things became really interesting when I began studying the financial markets rather than just designing new products. I started examining where I could take sensible risks so for example, I tried to work out whether the Central Bank would cut interest rates or whether the Chinese would flood the market with gold and so forth and I began to take small bets on the market and did very well. My confidence level started to grow and suddenly I was in a position where I was very quickly becoming a real risk-taker. It was a fascinating business and I seemed to have a flair for it. Before long I was making more money for the bank by betting on the market than I was from the derivatives. This did not go unnoticed and pretty soon I was established as the bank's top trader and was put in charge of a proprietary trading desk, where I would bet the bank's own money.

I was betting a lot on interest rates and on currencies and was using futures and options. I had a 24-hour desk staffed with economists and strategists so that we could always be watching the markets and I had to have total confidence in my intellect to figure out what might or might not happen and how it would affect the economy. I had come a long way, and by this time I really needed to believe in myself. I recall one of the most exciting occasions occurred when the Australian interest rates dropped to less than 10 per cent. Previously, they had been as high as 15 per cent, and even higher, but for some time I had been convinced that they would fall below 10 per cent. No one believed me, but I was confident in my predictions and I was positive that they would fall below that figure. I was isolated in this case but, happily, my view proved correct and I made the bank an incredible amount of money. It was also fun to win a lot of friendly bets I had made with my colleagues in the dealing room.

I look back on those times now and I can honestly say I have never experienced excitement like that in my life since. It was a brave new world and it was young traders who were taking over. Youth and dynamism and risk-taking were so important and I reached the point where I hated Friday afternoons because the markets were closed. In comparison to the hardship of my early childhood it seemed almost unbelievable. I recall earning $100,000 one year and I was delighted. I thought if I could lock that in for the rest of my life then it would be fantastic. I really did not think I needed any more than that and I could barely imagine earning a higher figure. It just seemed so improbable, so I kept saving and made the most of my good fortune, but then the next year I earned $500,000 and the following year $1 million and then $1.5 million. It was astounding. Money was everywhere and a lot of people who were earning less money than me were beginning to really enjoy themselves by buying Ferraris and Porsches and so forth. All that did not interest me. I was so thrilled to be recognised for my skills and felt a stark contrast to my upbringing, so I just thought I'd keep hold of most of my earnings and save for the future.

My success meant that I began to receive offers from all over the world. Eventually I accepted a request to manage a fund in Bermuda. At that time I have to admit that I did not even know where Bermuda was – I assumed it was in the Bahamas! This was an incredible deal – completely unbelievable. There was no choice but to accept it and the bank were distraught when I left. I worked in Bermuda for just two years believing that I had made enough money to retire. I took my family to Monaco and have been there ever since. I was 34 at this stage and although there was something in my head that told me I should go back to work, I still had that Aussie attitude inside me somewhere and I just wanted to relax and enjoy life.

That plan did not last very long! I became quite restless, even bored, so I started backing and investing in various companies. A friend of mine was an Oxford graduate and we became intrigued by the idea of taking business plans or products from universities and commercialising them. We thought it was a really under-exploited area. We knew that a lot of great ideas and products were just sitting and gathering dust at universities simply because of a lack of funds. There were real difficulties in moving from the research stage to the commercial stage and getting a product onto the market and achieving sales so that people could be paid to work for the company. I found it particularly fascinating to meet and talk with professors about new ideas and their research. We managed to maintain an arrangement that was extremely beneficial to all parties, with both the universities and me receiving some shares in any investments that I made in various businesses.

Thanks to contacts at Oxford I began backing a series of small business ideas which would prove to be both spellbinding and energising. It was not too dissimilar to what happens on *Dragons' Den* – trying to spot the best ideas and nurturing them with a combination of investment and expertise. I enjoyed it so much that I began investing in a large and diverse number of projects. Amongst others I acquired a diamond mine in Sierra Leone and

was the lead investor in the restoration of a Georgian materpiece –
Home House. Situated in London, Home House as a private
members club became a celebrity hang out for the likes of
Madonna and Paul McCartney.

As I intimated at the start, you could argue that I walked away
from investment banking at the wrong time, but the truth is that I
enjoy working with small businesses so much that I would never
change anything. I relish working with people and being able to
help change lives far more than looking at screens and studying
reports. For me it is the people that matter and I am proud that to
date I have helped over 70 companies with investments and advice.
Many of these are still works in progress but so far over 15 have
been sold to trade buyers or listed on the stock market. There is
one company in Scotland that I virtually held together for a while.
I did not even completely understand the technology, but they
were making microprocessors and now their chips are in the XBox
and the iPod. It is fun to look at businesses like that and wonder
whether the i-Pod would even exist if I had not kept faith in the
company. Some of the products I have backed from the universities are absolutely fundamental as well – treatment of cancer,
Alzheimer's disease, asthma, even acne, and it's fantastic to be
involved in these products that could hopefully change lives for
the better.

It is difficult for me to say how or why my career became a
success. I do know that I had a genuine desire to prove myself in
the work environment. Coming from my background, I wanted to

make something of myself and because I did not have any special connections or wealth to fall back on I realised that the only person I could rely on was myself. I suppose I was something of an outsider when I entered the world of the financial markets and I simply started from scratch. I did not read financial books or listen to other people's opinions – but formed my own ideas and attempted to figure things out for myself. I felt proud of what I achieved and also admired and respected all of my siblings who all now have great families. One brother was 14 when we were fostered and that has to be a devastating blow for someone of that age. Yet now he has a wonderful family and is a stationmaster in Melbourne, where he runs six stations. Everything has been tougher for him and I think his achievements are far greater than mine. Given the circumstances, just the fact he did not become some kind of criminal is a source of amazement!

Some might argue that my tough childhood spurred me on in some way, but all entrepreneurs are different. One has to be careful when attempting to analyse why some professional entrepreneurs are successful. In my case, perhaps I was incredibly lucky to be in the right places at the right times of my career; equally, other entrepreneurs may have simply launched their first product at the optimum time merely by chance, so analysing the many success stories may not reveal too many truths. In general, I do not think that there are any hard and fast rules about what makes an entrepreneur successful – what worked for one person may not be suitable for another.

Over the years I have really learnt to enjoy life. I'm into tennis, skiing and boating, and worked hard for 2 years recently writing a book called *100 Secret Strategies for Successful Investing*. I feel like my own character has turned full circle from my cautious formative years. I have almost become a deal junkie; I'm always looking for areas of risk that I can take. I get no thrill at all out of just watching a market go up or down – and I always distinguish between sensible risk and outright gambling. My kick comes from calculating whether a particular product or company is a good risk. I know that the failure rate in small businesses is tremendously high, but I will take risks on these businesses if I believe in the people running them and if they are enjoyable to work with over time the successes should outweigh the failures if I can do my job well. And on top of that, I can have a lot of enjoyment along the way changing peoples lives and creating new products.

PART 2
INSIDE THE DEN

When you see the Dragons in the Den you quickly realise that they choose their investments using completely different criteria – one Dragon will see potential that another totally misses. That's because the Dragons have different ideas about what will make a success.

Theo cares about the business plan, and the operations management of the business. From Theo you will learn how retail works and when investment is really needed. His case studies show two completely different ideas – one he invested in, and one he rejected. Theo knew that Gavin Wheeldon's translation business was good. Gavin had prepared a perfect pitch – but Theo astutely saw that Gavin didn't need investment. In the Foldio case study we learn how Theo was 'blown away' by Christian Lane's business idea and he knew that he could help retail part of his business. Here the key business lesson is that having a patent is important if you have a completely new product.

Duncan is a man of passion. It is the people he likes that get his investment. While the other Dragons did not see potential in Denise Hutton's Razzamataz, Duncan knew it could become a successful franchise business. The Razzamataz case study shows how, with help, a small business can become an international franchise. Not all businesses receive the investment they want, and Peter Ashley's Multi-Gym case study was a failure in the Den. Peter's product was not properly developed, and even though Duncan runs health clubs he did not want to invest – but it is still one of Duncan's favourite Den experiences.

Deborah's style in the Den seems rather fierce, but when you read her case studies you see how much she cares about her customers and their experience of the products that she has invested in. You will read in the MixAlbum case study just how as soon as she met Ian Chamings and visited the office of MixAlbum with fellow invester Theo Paphitis, she wanted to improve the customer experience on his website. This case study shows how entrepreneurs need a wide range of skills – Ian is an engineer and a patent lawyer; he just needed marketing expertise. Deborah brought more than just money to his business; she brought her experience and expertise in marketing. However, Deborah did not proceed with her planned investment in KC Jones' hi-tech sanitising unit, Klenz. His case study shows the importance of having all the details of the business ready for the investors. Even if you have interest from an investor there is still 'due diligence' to be endured. The investor will want to know every detail before the deal is finally signed.

Peter Jones loves hi-tech investments, so it was surprising that he fell for the singing Levi Roots along with Richard Farleigh, but then

Peter knew how to get Levi's Reggae Reggae Sauce into the stores. Levi's case study is already a Dragons' Den legend, because it shows how some business ideas can break all the rules and still be successful. Peter's other moneymaking investment follows a more traditional business plan. Imran Hakim was already a successful entrepreneur when he came into the Den with iTeddy – his business plan was based on vision and detailed business knowledge, and now his hard work has won the day. Peter made this investment along with Theo Paphitis.

So how will James invest? He tells us that he would have 'passed' on Reggae Reggae Sauce, but would have liked to join Richard and Duncan with Igloo Thermo-Logistics. He is looking for people who swim against the stream: his business ethos is 'observe the masses and do the opposite'.

Richard is the man who understands finance better than anyone, he is less interested in if the business plan can stack up, and more interested in the people and the idea. So he invested in Levi Roots, and would have liked to join Ling Valentine if only she had offered a bigger percentage of her business in return for the investment. Richard looked carefully at the proposal from Anthony Coates-Smith and Alistair Turner because he was aware that it is difficult to turn a commodity service into a niche business, but the two 'cool dudes' knew their business. They are now super-successful and expanding, and Richard and Duncan are helping their growth.

PETER JONES

Peter Jones is notorious for his competitive style and incredible business vision. He makes decisions quickly when he is in the Den, and enjoys the excitement of bidding against his fellow Dragons. He has a very sharp mind, is incredibly quick witted and is known for his many one-liners that have become part of Dragons' Den *legend.*

When someone comes up the stairs into the Den I look first at their presentation – how they look, how they speak, how concise they are, are they getting the key messages about their product or their service across? Then in my head I quickly run through a few key business questions: What's the financial opportunity behind the business? Have they evaluated risk? How much have they researched their product? What's their previous history? How much experience have they had in this market before? My brain is working on a quick 'snapshot'. Probably 20 thoughts go round in my head in the first three minutes although it takes me less than a minute to work out whether something is worth my pursuing.

I don't want to ask too many key questions at first, because I would just be giving information to the other Dragons. I wait for the other Dragons to say they are out before I ask some of the crucial questions that turn the investment on its head and might make me really want to invest. I am playing against the other Dragons because if it is a great business opportunity I don't want them to get it.

When I am in the Den I come up with a lot of one-liners and people think I plan them in advance, but I don't – there's a lot of joking around and I just come out with them, and what's funny is that radio stations replay them. In this new series we are filming at Pinewood Studios and it is a much better location for us. We have a big room we can relax in, with soft chairs and television. We don't get much time off, we start early and finish late, but when we do have a break it's comfortable.

I get on well with the other Dragons. Theo is very sharp and intelligent. He's my biggest competition in the Den. He's a proven recovery specialist – he can turn around a business in a heartbeat and not many people have that talent. He's probably one of the leading entrepreneurs in this country. If Theo is angling to get in on the action you know you are in for a bit of a ride, because he's a tough competitor, but we work well together. We know what we want. He's a good planner like me and we both like to plan for success. We like to focus on the key elements of the business and find different ways to enhance it and get underneath the bonnet. We have regular board meetings and it is a real pleasure to work with him; he's a very good guy. He's also very humorous.

Duncan and I have worked together on *Dragons' Den* since the start and are the only remaining Dragons from the first series. He has clearly done very well, he's built businesses, and made a lot of money. I do struggle sometimes to work out where he's coming from. Some of the questions he asks are just strange to me, and maybe that's what makes us different: he can obviously see opportunities that I just can't see. Contrary to public belief we do get on off-camera. He is genuinely good fun to be with. And *Dragons' Den* wouldn't be the same without him. We have been working together on a child safety seat. Peter Sesay came into the Den for financial help with the production of his Autosafe seat-belt adjuster, designed to improve the comfort and safety of children in booster car seats. Duncan was so impressed with the seat-belt adjuster that he was willing to offer half the £100,000 Peter was after, and I invested the other half. My team is currently looking at how we can get Autosafe into retailers. It's a tough investment but it covers an area that is really interesting for both of us. If it takes off it will not only save lives but we also believe a lot of people will buy it.

I think Deborah's quite different in reality from how she appears on the programme – she seems very fierce on the show, but actually it couldn't be further from the truth: she's a lovely lady. She's incredibly knowledgeable, she understands the business straight away, she always asks the right questions, and she makes her decisions very quickly. She's concise, but she knows what she's talking about, and that's what makes her great on that programme because she has brilliant instincts. She is right almost all of the time and she nails it.

Richard is a nice guy. He made a real effort on the show; he certainly put his money on the table. I have got one business with him in Reggae Reggae Sauce. He really knows the economics of business, and he is also very analytical.

James Caan is very smart. He's the perfect choice to be a Dragon. He's got that gentlemanly image, very softly spoken, but I am sure that I am going to see a little bit more of the feistiness and the bite in him. He seems a very astute investor and I like the fact that he is a venture capitalist for real. He took to filming like a duck to water. He just got into the flow straight away.

I think Evan is brilliant. He's first class, I even watch him on the news. He's clearly one of the most intellectual economists in this country and I think *Dragons' Den* has been a learning curve for him, just as it has been for us from a TV perspective. I think his view was originally very theoretical, whereas now he sees that there are possibilities in things that don't look promising. I have described Evan as a weather man: 80 per cent of the time he gets it right by applying theory and figures, but there are a few times when he gets it wrong. Needless to say, like all of us Dragons, he seems to have acquired more expensive suits since the series started!

In the Den we have had some surprising entrepreneurs. I will never forget Peter Ashley – he was the man who invented an exercise machine that fell apart. You will remember that Duncan tried it out, and I said it was like 'two old codgers' trying to 'get fit' in their living room. Although at first sight it seemed a ridiculous idea, I think now that Peter Ashley could probably take it a stage further. Maybe he should re-model the product as more of a fitness chair – something that supports your back, and your posture, and then you do your exercises. With a slightly different twist the Dragons might have been interested. On the other hand I just couldn't see the attraction behind the right-hand glove to aid safe driving abroad; my view is that if you can remember to put a golf glove on I am sure you are going to remember which side of the road to drive on.

I don't look back at any investments in *Dragons' Den* and regret not having got involved. I am proud of the fact that I invested in *Wonderland* magazine. I own 40 per cent of it and *Wonderland* is still going strong today when most magazines fail in the first year, and 85 per cent fail by year two.

As soon as Levi Roots was halfway up the stairs, his singing made me smile. I didn't have a clue about the product. I thought he was radiant and engaging. I couldn't wait to know what his product actually was. He really got me, hook, line and sinker; I was totally engaged. It was a unique, compelling start to a pitch. I always want to touch, feel, taste and see, do a consumer test, and I liked the sauce. I thought it was going to blow my head off, but it didn't – Reggae Reggae Sauce is quite mild and it tasted fantastic, and from that moment I was sold, even though Levi got his sales projections wrong. Now he has proved everybody else wrong. Even though he made a mistake adding up the quantities he believed he could sell, he has now actually sold that quantity, so he was right all along!

The very next morning after the programme was broadcast I was on the telephone to the Chief Executive of Sainsbury's. I sold Levi's product over the phone, we had a meeting that afternoon with his team, and three weeks later we had bottles in every one of Sainsbury's stores. What I could add to Levi's integrity and delicious sauce were my contacts, my knowledge of how to sell and the management of the sale, so the end-to-end commercial transaction was done by me. The sauce has achieved cult status in this country, outselling tomato ketchup. Levi's is an amazing success story and because of his success with the sauce he has been able to follow his dream and opened a restaurant called Rastarant. And he didn't need us to back it.

Imran Hakim was incredible – the way that he put his pitch across using his brother in the teddy outfit for a live demonstration. What impressed me was that he had a clear vision for his business. He saw that iTeddy could be the next best-selling toy for children at Christmas and he took us on a journey to show why it would be very successful.

He demonstrated that he had a product and a web development tool; he showed us, gave us figures of what he thought he could achieve, told us whom he thought he could sell it to and who would buy it. He told us why the consumers would want it, and he gave us an example of why in the future iTeddy would be even more successful, because it would be based around downloads directly to the device.

For me it was an absolutely simple investment and I couldn't wait to negotiate the deal and get my money off the table into his pocket. I was delighted.

There have been a great many changes in the design and product plans and the iTeddy has developed. Theo is a real techie; he loves gadgets. He would query everything: 'What about this USB, let's change that, let's have a look at this.' Imran was always quick to respond – 'OK, I am going to go back to China to get those things changed.' In other business environments you might expect the executive to leave for China to see the change in the next couple of weeks but Imran would go to China that afternoon! He would have the changes made within three days and he would be back before the end of the week. His focus and determination are astonishing and that's why Imran is a true entrepreneur. He has an initial order of 35,000 products with Argos and I'm sure it is going to be their best-selling product this Christmas.

Theo persuaded me to get dressed up as an iTeddy at London Zoo to launch the product. It was worth it.

PETER JONES' DRAGONS' RULES FOR SUCCESS

● **VISION** If you're going to dream, dream big. One horizon always reveals another.

● **INFLUENCE** There are times when all entrepreneurs need others. Influence is twinned with win-win.

● **CONFIDENCE** An inner self-belief is like a cornerstone under the tallest building. There is no such thing as failure, only feedback.

● **TAKE ACTION** Most successful entrepreneurs understand that action is just like a powerful drug. Entrepreneurs make things happen.

A LESSON THAT BREAKS ALL THE RULES OF BUSINESS:
LEVI ROOTS' REGGAE REGGAE SAUCE

As the episode began, reggae singer Levi Roots strummed his way into the Dragons' Den *with a few jars of his home-made spicy sauce. It had proved to be popular at the Notting Hill carnival, and he wanted to start producing it on a commercial scale. He was looking for £50,000 for a 20 per cent share of his business. Levi's story breaks all the rules of business.*

He arrived on the show with no business plan, not even a sheet of numbers. Instead, he brought his guitar and a simple song:

> *Put some music in my food for me and give me some Reggae*
> *Reggae Sauce.*
> *Hot Reggae Reggae Sauce, it's so nice, I had to name it twice,*
> *I called it Reggae Reggae Sauce.*
> *Just like my baby it's the perfect delight,*
> *It's got some peppers and some herbs and spice …*

This was not an approach likely to succeed with a bank manager, nor even a speculative venture capital company. Levi was well aware that the Dragons' Den was probably the only place where he could pull a stunt like this and get away with it. What Levi's experience in the Den proves is that some businesses that break all the rules can still be winners.

The Dragons enjoyed the opening gambit but they were less impressed when it transpired that Levi had misinterpreted a letter from his first potential major buyer. While he enthusiastically claimed to have in his pocket a firm order from a meat company in Yorkshire for, wait for it, 2.5 million litres of sauce, which would generate turnover of £16.25 million, what the letter actually envisaged was an initial requirement of 2,500 kilos, followed by potential orders worth about £130,000 in turnover per year.

When Richard Farleigh unearthed this disastrous miscalculation, Levi was unabashed, even defiant. Unashamed of his weakness in finance and accounting, his instincts told him to play to his strengths, and he knows where his strengths lie. 'I am a singer, I am a song writer, I am a sauce man, I am a performer. I am not a mathematician and if I am going to use your money, your well hard-earned money, in my business, I am going to employ the best accountant there is to look after that. Don't ask me anything about it!'

Duncan Bannatyne thought the business wouldn't make money, Deborah Meaden was concerned that Levi had no concept of what it would take to produce the quantities of sauce that he was talking about but in any event considered it a lifestyle option for the owner, and Theo Paphitis said that Levi should be able to manage without outside investment if he could bring the orders he already had to fruition. After outright rejections from these three, Levi was staring failure in the face.

So he hesitated for just a few seconds before accepting offers from Peter Jones and Richard Farleigh to invest the money he needed, in return for double the equity percentage he had offered. The deal left Levi with 60 per cent of an embryonic business which was now valued at £125,000, equivalent to 33 times the previous year's turnover. But this was not the sort of calculation Levi was likely to make for himself.

Although Levi – it's a pseudonym, his real name is Keith – is happy to be a celebrity, the sauce business is not show business. To succeed, he knows he will need to draw on other strengths as well.

First, Reggae Reggae Sauce is a good product. The recipe is a closely guarded secret, but it is a hot-to-mild, jerk, barbecue sauce – an alternative to tomato ketchup and hot pepper relish. Levi thinks he has spotted a gap in the market: ketchup tastes only of tomato, while hot pepper relish is, well, hot – it tastes only of pepper. His sauce, he says, retains the flavours of the garlic, peppers, coriander, scallions and all the herbs and spices it contains.

Levi learned all about Jamaican food as a child. His mother and grandmother taught him how to cook in their own style: traditional dishes like rice and peas and ackee, swordfish, and jerk chicken. In Jamaica, they made everything from scratch, using the fresh vegetables they grew in their garden and wild yams from the fields.

Second, he has researched the production side of the business and knows what it will take to switch from cottage industry to mass production. Although he started making the sauce in small quantities in his tiny kitchen at home with his children helping him, one of the first things he did was to get the necessary approval from the Food Standards Agency to enable him to sell it legally. And he was not daunted by the prospect of renting factory premises and investing £25,000 in equipment in order to scale up.

Third, and perhaps most importantly, Levi has the resilience and the determination he will need to succeed as an entrepreneur. He has his own way of explaining where these personal qualities came from. His life story begins, as he sees it, when his parents left Jamaica for the UK to look for work in the 1950s. Levi was seven or eight years old, and he was left behind. His parents' departure is his first memory and the image of it is still vivid in his mind. Levi's mother found work and sent for his five brothers and sisters one at a time, but Levi, being the youngest, stayed on at home with his grandmother for four years. Coming to terms with his parents' decision to leave him, understanding that it had to be done, was Levi's first major challenge. It came at a very early age, but he faced up to it. The family was too poor to send him to school but his grandmother taught him everything she knew about Christianity, talked to him about music – she was a singer in the Baptist Church and had a fantastic voice – and taught him how to sing. Levi believes it was during this time in Jamaica that he became who he is.

The next major challenge was moving to the UK at the age of 12. Levi arrived in winter, and remembers finding himself in a scary place where the leafless trees looked as though they had hands instead of branches, so different from the evergreens back home. Everything looked dull, and he missed his grandmother terribly. Levi knew how to look after himself and keep house, but he could not read or write, or even spell his name. He could only count from one to ten. He found school a hostile environment and did not learn anything there, so his mother taught him herself, which meant spending three or four hours in the local library with him every evening.

As well as teaching him to read and write, to sing and do maths, his mother told him about slavery, and what it meant to be black, and this was the time when he started listening to reggae music. It was the era of Bob Marley, Burning Spear and Dennis Brown. Their music was a conduit for news about Jamaica, Rastafarianism, blackness and African origins, and it helped Levi to have an insight into his own identity.

Well before Levi left school at 16, he had moved to the front of the class and excelled in English, Geography and English literature. He reckons he was well educated, and his first job was as an engineer, but at 17 the music called him away – he felt it ran in his blood – and he joined a sound system in Brixton, South London called Sir Coxon, and toured the country with it, playing at all the clubs, mixing with superstars like the Rolling Stones and the Beatles.

A lucky break came in 1981, when the owner of the sound system offered to produce Levi's first song, called 'Poor Man's Story', and the following year he formed his own band, Matic 1. It was a big success in the early 1980s, well known for playing UK reggae, as opposed to Jamaican, with a focus on 'roots' music in the spiritual tradition of Bob Marley and the Wailers.

Levi seems to have a natural talent for marketing. When he first started selling food at the Notting Hill carnival in 1992, he called his stall 'Rastaurant' and it went from strength to strength. Every year for 15 years, Levi would act crazy and sing while the customers were served, and all the food came with Reggae Reggae Sauce on top. People took liberal helpings of it home in empty bottles and jam-jars, and this spontaneous kind of promotion built up its reputation.

Levi stuck to singing until he got fed up with people telling him that they wanted the sauce and he realised he could achieve success in the food business – but only if he gave up the music. It was a tough decision, not taken lightly after 30 years in the world of music, but Levi knew it was a sacrifice he had to make.

The sauce was named and formally launched at carnival in 2006, in bottles with proper labels. Levi applied for a start-up loan from GLE1, a company set up by the Mayor of London to help small businesses to get off the ground, and met with one of their mentors who pointed him in the direction of the right food exhibitions for his product. One of them was the World Food Market in London's Docklands. It cost Levi about £1,200 to exhibit there – more than the £1,000 he had borrowed from the Mayor's small business fund – but the risk paid off. It was while he was there selling his sauce and singing his song that a researcher from *Dragons' Den* tapped him on the shoulder and asked him if he was looking for investment.

Levi had never watched the programme. He thought it was a soap opera until he went home and asked his kids about it. They had seen the programme, but they advised their father against taking part because, they said, 'No Rasta man with five-inch dreadlocks singing a guitar about a sauce ain't going to get investment.' Because they felt he stood no chance, they did not want him to compete.

It was Levi's mother who swung the balance the other way. 'She said, "Look, you have been doing this sauce for so long, believe in yourself!" She told me what to say in my prayers and to go and read Psalm 23, which tells you "The Lord is My Shepherd, I shall not want". And she said, "Son, you have been wanting a long time. So go to your Shepherd and say you have been wanting a long time. Stop the wanting!" So when I was coming up the stairs of the Dragons' Den, all that was in my head really was what she had told me. And I just had that faith, which she had in me, and I just went.'

Levi's strategy for the show was to be different from all the other contenders. Rather than try to sound convincing by talking numbers, he decided to rely on his talent as a performer and his experience in marketing the sauce, and to use his song as his weapon to slay the Dragons. 'I decided not to take any numbers. I thought, "To hell with it." My prayer, my song and my guitar were the three things I had. And I came through.'

When Evan Davis pointed out to him that his numbers were all over the place and that a lot of people on the programme get grilled and humiliated when they don't know the numbers, Levi responded with a broad grin, 'Well, I got it from my mother. My mother yesterday she told me to come here and knock 'em dead! and I tried to do that. She said, "Go and do it and you will come back a dragon slayer!"'

The main benefit of the show to Levi, apart from a £50,000 cash injection, has been the acquisition of two highly influential investors. Peter Jones has helped with many aspects of the business, including guest appearances on TV and radio interviews, and just a few days after the programme was aired, he introduced Levi to Sainsbury's CEO, Justin King. Three weeks later, Levi had signed a six-month exclusive contract with the supermarket, and Reggae Reggae Sauce was on the shelves in every store. Production moved to a factory in Wales, employing 18 people at the outset. The first batch was 150,000 bottles, a far cry from the 65 at a time he was able to churn out in his own kitchen in Brixton.

Levi was more than happy to follow Peter Jones's lead in negotiating his first major deal. He was also jubilant about the publicity that came his way. 'It is just fantastic. I really didn't think something like this could happen to a black guy playing music about a sauce on the telly. It is just absolutely out of this world. Every morning I wake up and I see the hundreds of e-mails I get, and it strikes me even more, what an extraordinary thing has really happened.'

But his ambitions for the company extend far beyond this stage. As well as four different flavours of the sauce, he has plans for pizzas and a range of meat products, including jerk chicken and curried goat, and he is keeping his options open with regard to distribution when the six-month exclusive contract with Sainsbury's expires.

Although he is ambitious, Levi is too pragmatic to indulge in daydreams. His realism is based in a homespun philosophy which matches his home-cooked products. Asked if he was happy after accepting the Dragons' offer that cost him 40 per cent of his equity, he said he was over the moon, but then added, 'I mean you don't usually get exactly what you want in this world, but you have to make do with the little that you have.'

Levi does not delude himself that customers in the mass market will initially buy his product for its flavour. Unlike the punters at the Notting Hill carnival, supermarket shoppers will not have a chance to taste it before piling it into their trolleys. They will be buying his brand. The thousands of people who visit Levi's website say they like what they see. They have never tried his sauce but they have seen *him*. Peter Jones also knows that it is not the sauce that is selling, at this point, but Levi's personality. He seems to be somebody people can relate to, somebody who persuades them to trust Caribbean food if they've never tried it before. 'Peter and Richard saw that with me and my personality, I didn't have to change because I didn't come pretending that I knew anything. I just came as myself and this is what the British public liked. Nobody has got to tell me anything really. I just go and just do what I do, which is be Levi Roots.'

And his advice to other would-be entrepreneurs? 'Try and shove a square thing in a round hole sometimes because if you don't do that you never try new things! A lot of people wouldn't have gone on the show because of the stereotypical type of winners who are normally on, and because they were sure that black people were not going to win. But my attitude was that you have got to be in it to win it. And I decided to be in it, and I won it.'

A LESSON IN ENTHUSIASM AND BUSINESS VISION:
IMRAN HAKIM'S iTEDDY

'Your mind and your time: that's the key to any entrepreneur's success.'

Looking back now on his experience in the Dragons' Den, 29-year-old Imran Hakim from Bolton can afford to sound proud of what he has achieved. 'What the Dragons taught me is that sometimes what you lack in resources, you can more than make up with the level of your enthusiasm and your energy.'

Imran's concept, iTeddy, was presented to the Den in the fourth series. The original idea had come out of a conversation with his younger brother, Zubair, in which the two young men were vying to see who could come up with the best idea for a gift for Imran's young niece. His idea shows that new technology offers good scope for investors.

'iTeddy brings the teddy bear into the 21st century' is how he described it to the Dragons. A soft toy with a screen in its belly, Imran's concept turned the teddy into a personal media player with a simple, child-friendly user interface, and generated further revenue by setting up an accompanying website from which licensed content, entertainment or educational, could be downloaded. The child can then decide for him or herself which cartoons to watch, or take iTeddy to bed and, via an audio function, choose to play themselves a favourite bedtime story.

Imran already had a strong track record as an entrepreneur. Since his early teens, he always knew that he wanted to be in charge of his own business. At 15, wanting to upgrade his computer system to be able to play the latest games, he discovered that he could make a profit by selling his old machine for more than it had cost to buy. He borrowed £2,000 from his father, and set himself up to supply computers to his school teachers. By spotting that this was the right moment to seize the opportunity presented by an emerging technology, within only a week he had made enough to pay his father back.

'People weren't as familiar with computers then. The initial adopters were using PCs, but the market wasn't really saturated, and there was no real mass-market awareness. Companies like PC World or Tiny, who came to dominate the market in the following decade, were not yet well known, and so people weren't as price sensitive as they are today. They simply wanted a product that was easy to use and was accessible, so it was a great time for independent and individual computer component assemblers to make good margins in the computer market.'

Imran could have gone on to develop his computer-supply business further, but instead he trained as an optometrist, using the money he had made continuing to sell computers during his student days to teachers and friends to set up his first optician's practice in Bolton before he had even qualified. He employed a friend to perform eye-tests, diversified into a recruitment agency supplying locum optometrists to other practices, built a group of independent practices around the Northwest, and eventually also bought out a frame distribution company and a lens laboratory to service both his own shops and others throughout the country.

So what made him come up with the concept of iTeddy as a toy for a child like his niece? 'It's a classic gift, but with MP3/MP4 electronic functionality so that children can choose what they want to watch or listen to on the teddy itself. My family said they thought it was bound to have been done already, and if it hadn't, then clearly that was because it was a lame idea that wouldn't work, but the more I thought about it, the more possibilities I saw. I imagined a download aspect to it – setting up a website to provide licensed content – and realised that there would be an additional revenue stream that could be generated from that. Essentially it was an invention that offered a number of revenue streams, on-line and off-line.'

Convinced his idea had possibilities, Imran went on the internet to search what might already be out there. 'When I realised no one had yet developed this concept I decapitated one of my niece's little teddies and integrated some MP3 gadgetry. The prototype was a bit of a monstrosity, but at least it gave some indication of what might be achieved. I took it to a friend, Riaz, who owns a marketing and design company, and asked him to put together some visuals.'

Armed only with this idea and a two-dimensional drawing, Imran's enthusiasm persuaded the producers of *Dragons' Den* to give him a chance to enter the Den when they met him in Manchester at a business-to-business networking event. Imran was at first reluctant to pitch such a sketchy notion in front of the audition cameras. 'I asked how long I would have to talk for and was told maybe three minutes. I thought: what on earth can I say for three minutes about a drawing on a piece of paper? But about eight minutes later they had to drag me off camera saying, "Yes, that's enough, we get the picture."'

Between this audition and the actual filming date, far from sitting back satisfied, Imran was busier than ever laying the groundwork for iTeddy. He used his connections at Manchester University to get access to market-research reports on the latest developments in the toy industry, the personal-media-player business and the download market, all of which confirmed his initial hunch that this was an emerging market, and iTeddy represented the direction in which children's toys were moving. 'Kids are getting older younger. They crave the same kind of technology enjoyed by their older brothers and sisters. Even long-established toys like Action Man and Barbie are beginning to include some sort of electronic functionality.' While in the Far East on business connected with his chain of opticians, he had a prototype made of iTeddy, so he would have something physical to show the Dragons.

In the Den, accompanied by his brother dressed as a teddy bear with a screen in its middle, Imran looked calm, confident and well prepared. He knew he'd put the work in, believed he had a great product, and was determined to succeed. 'I'm looking for an investment of £140,000 in return for a 15 per cent share in the business,' he told the Dragons.

'Do you own intellectual rights to this?' was Theo Paphitis's first question.

'We have a patent pending, which covers the actual idea of a personal media player being incorporated within a soft toy,' Imran replied. The question of whether or not his patent application would be successful turned out to be key in the Dragons' initial response to his idea.

Deborah Meaden was yet to be convinced. Although the patent agent had told Imran there was a good chance the patent would be granted, she felt that iTeddy could be vulnerable to copycat rivals. Richard Farleigh too was unhappy about the patent situation. His instincts were telling him that whatever the lawyers said, the patent was far from within Imran's grasp, and he had a hunch that in the end Imran might not get it after all. And right from the start, Duncan Bannatyne hated the whole idea.

'You've made me so sad,' he told Imran. 'Reading bedtime stories to the child is a father's job. I don't want to be replaced by a teddy bear. This idea really depresses me. I don't think we should encourage joining technology and teddies together … I hope it doesn't work for you. I'm out.'

It was a crushing blow, but the young entrepreneur refused to let it throw him. Theo Paphitis had been encouraging; and Imran thought he might have another Dragon almost hooked. Peter Jones had initially been sceptical when he saw Imran walk into the Den with a teddy bear, but he was impressed by the enthusiasm and professionalism of his presentation. His immediate response was to want to drill down into the potential profitability of iTeddy, and he demanded figures. Imran was well prepared for this, and able to project margins right through his distribution chain.

'We are looking to sell into retailers and on the Internet and expect the high-street price to be between £45 and £55.'

'I liked the amount of energy he'd put into really thinking this idea through,' Peter Jones says now.

Peter offered to put up half the £140,000 Imran needed, in return for a 22.5 per cent share and Theo Paphitis chipped in immediately to match Peter's offer, conditional on the patent application being successful, but this meant giving away 45 per cent of his business to them. Imran wavered for a moment, hoping he might do better, if other Dragons were still interested. But with Duncan already out, both Deborah and Richard shook their heads. Imran realised he would not get anything like the investment he needed by insisting on keeping to his original 15 per cent equity offer. He managed to keep his cool and negotiate the two inter-ested Dragons down to 40 per cent – a high-risk strategy, but one that paid off.

'I realised that apart from the investment itself, what I was getting was the chance to see what it is these guys do that is so different, and what makes them so successful,' he explains. 'The product is so much better today than it was initially, that I can only wonder what on earth was I thinking when I was so proud of the prototype I brought to the Den.'

Only 15 minutes after the show, Imran was getting the benefit of the Jones/Paphitis experience. Peter and Theo wasted no time in making their first suggestion to improve iTeddy – making the personal media player removable, so that the child could keep its beloved teddy if it became necessary to upgrade the central unit, or even just wash the bear.

'Straight from day one they took a real interest in the intimate details of the product design,' says Imran. 'For instance, they suggested later I should change the look of the bear.' The proto-type had been made up in the Far East, and Theo thought it looked too Chinese. To sell in the British market, it needed to look and feel more Western. 'The point he made was that the hype and publicity will sell the product to an extent, but it's the *quality* of design and manufacture that will really get people excited, and that will help create the long-term brand.'

After the show, the first task was to draw up contracts. A patent ruling can take up to four years to come through, and with that in mind, the Dragons took the view that it was worth laying out money immediately on iTeddy, or the opportunity could be lost. Even if the patent was not granted in the long run, there was a virtue in being first to market.

Imran was encouraged by the Dragons to take iTeddy to the 2007 Toy Fair. The toy generated a massive amount of excitement there. Imran had approaches from a number of industry majors, Toys"R"Us, Argos and Hamleys among them. Companies from all over the world stopped at his stand to express an interest in the distribution rights.

'The day *Dragons' Den* aired, I was in a meeting with Argos. It was a wonderful feeling to be able to tell their buyer to watch out for the programme that evening. We knew we would get some website traffic as a result of the broadcast, but we could never have predicted how much. Our server crashed because we were getting something like 400 hits a second. The response was overwhelming. The following day there were thousands of e-mails, from companies offering marketing ideas, business services, or people asking when they could buy it.'

iTeddy was delivered to market in summer 2007, listed as a top-ten toy by its retailers. It has been a remarkably rapid progress from the initial idea to a product on the shelf. So how does Imran feel the Dragons' involvement expedited the process?

'They're not there to run your business. Their aim is to see that you are geared up and motivated to drive the business forward yourself, but if they see enthusiasm coming from you, it makes them more inclined to offer more of their time and resources. I've been amazed at how much they've given me.' Imran is in e-mail or phone contact with Peter or Theo more or less every other day – they meet sometimes twice a week. He cherishes the wisdom they bring to his business.

'From the very first meeting we had together, it was apparent that in every statement they make there is probably a lesson it would otherwise take you six months to learn by yourself. For instance, I remember Theo asking me about the tax-efficient set-up of my other business interests, and my response was perhaps a little wishy-washy – after all, I reckoned I have a Financial Director and tax advisers whom I pay to do that sort of thinking for me. Theo rounded on me immediately. 'Imran, that's a poor answer,' he said. 'It could be costing your company a lot of money. You need to be an expert in every part of your own business. How are you going to question your Financial Director if you yourself don't intimately understand what it is that you are directing him to do?'

Running a business takes time and energy. As Imran has discovered, launching a brand new product takes even more. It is not easy knowing that friends of his own age are out having fun while he pores over spreadsheets, his life dictated by the rigours of a production cycle and delivery schedules. He appreciates that he is lucky to have had so much of the Dragons' time and enthusiasm, and therefore his policy is to make the most of every moment, preparing thoroughly for every meeting, setting clear objectives for what he hopes to achieve, so that every minute spent with his backers counts.

'Managing time efficiently has definitely been the key to being where we are right now with iTeddy, and has expedited how fast we have moved – vital when the aim is to be first to market with a new idea. I think our biggest difficulty has been trying to make a decision on which of the many offers on the table will be the right strategic move for iTeddy's future. When there is such a wealth of opportunities, from all over the world, it's easy to get carried away, but we have to be sure that we are steady walking before we start running.'

It was Imran's energy and enthusiasm that attracted both Dragons. 'I've said more than once that entrepreneurship is the rock'n'roll of the modern day,' says Peter Jones. 'And in those terms, Imran has the potential to be a real star, but what I like about him is his willingness to learn. I tell him that there is no such thing as failure, only feedback. If you try something the first time and it doesn't work, you shouldn't let yourself be disheartened – take a lesson from it and let it fuel your drive to do better next time. He's a young man with his feet on the ground, and although he stands to make a great deal of money if iTeddy is a success, it isn't money that motivates him. It's the sheer joy of doing what he does – and if that's the way you approach business, it will take you a long way towards success.'

Imran agrees. 'If money is your sole motivation, business can become a lonely path very, very quickly. For me, it's the sense of achievement that comes from an idea popping into my head, developing it with a team of people and finally seeing it on a retail shelf – that gives me *real* satisfaction. When I look back over the last ten years, what matters is not where I find myself right now, exciting as the opportunities that lie ahead are, but the journey that brought me here, the obstacles I've overcome and the people

I work with. That's what really puts a big smile on my face: it makes all the sleepless nights, the dilemmas, and the hard work worthwhile.'

DEBORAH MEADEN

Deborah's business style in the Den is formal and formidable, but she has a heart of gold and once she has found a firm she wants to invest in, she brings her excellent marketing expertise into play, and a golden touch that can transform its fortunes.

I joined the *Dragons' Den* for the third series; I'd turned down offers of television work in the past and I certainly don't regard myself as a media 'natural'. I hated the publicity photographs – like many people, I forget that I'm not 23 any more! I watched the first episode of *Dragons' Den* on the sofa with my husband, peeping through my fingers.

I consider my stint in the Den in the same way I consider life in general. It's the job I'm doing at the moment. I'm enjoying it and I'm having a lot of fun, but I do actually have a job to do. I think I'm quite level-headed – it's my practical no-nonsense approach, as much as my expertise in sales and marketing, that make me effective in the Den.

As the only female Dragon, I get asked a lot of questions about what it's like to be a woman in a man's world. Of course, I don't perceive the world of business as a 'man's world', but it seems that other people do. I think it's all a bit daft. I try to ignore the male/female thing – I avoid playing the gender card. If somebody else has issues about my being a woman, they had better deal with it. If anyone wants to do business with me, they need to know that I'm not interested in the gender question. My own mother is very strong; she started with nothing and she is now very successful, so I suppose I get my confidence from her. I don't set out to be a role model, but if women wanting to go into the world of business are inspired or encouraged by my success, then that's great.

I think I have lots of self-awareness and self-belief and this is what underpins my career. On the television I know I come across as hard, but really I'm only rational and businesslike. When I concentrate, my face is deadpan; when I'm making business decisions I can be quite dispassionate because you have to be, but I've got more humour than most people would think. I work in the leisure industry for goodness sake. If I didn't know how to have fun, I wouldn't be very good at providing it!

I know I don't suffer fools gladly, and one of my faults is that I can be too blunt at times. That comes across on television, but obviously it's a concentrated version of me. I'm not going to apologise for saying what I think when somebody presents me with a flawed business idea. It's irresponsible not to be straight with people – there's so much at stake. You simply cannot tell someone strongly enough, particularly when you can see in their eyes that they are not going to take a gentle hint – you're going to have to smack them round the face with it.

Maybe my honesty can seem brutal in the Den, but honesty is a fundamental principle in my own life. I like people to be clear and straightforward. I will not invest with somebody I do not trust. I'm quite happy for someone to admit that they are not very competent or strong in a certain area, and that's why they need help. That's fine, if they're truthful about it and listen to the advice that's offered. I like dealing with people who can stand their ground – someone who will question, or be brave if questions are fired at them. The world of business is a very tough world, and I have to be sure that someone I invest with is not going to crumble under pressure. On the other hand, I'm well aware that the atmosphere of the Den is pretty hot and it's not a place where people are going to feel relaxed. There are very few people who won't show signs of tension, so I cut them some slack, but not too much, because if they can't stand up to scrutiny in the Den they're not going to last long in the world of business.

First impressions are extremely important, as they are in all aspects of life. I ask myself: Is there eye contact? Is there confidence? Do they believe in their product? Do they know their stuff? Usually, I can sum all that up pretty quickly.

If the candidate survives the initial baptism of fire and convinces me that they would be capable of withstanding pressure and pulling a business through the bad times, they then need to show me that they've done proper research. Can they convince me that they know enough about their chosen market? Have they addressed that market? What's unique about their product? Why are customers going to switch from currently successful products over to their product?

I'm looking for people who have a grasp on *why*. Too many people think that they're going to succeed solely through clever advertising and publicity, but no matter how great your publicity, ultimately you have to have a good, value for money product and be able to deliver the goods. What you're offering has to have real quality. So what I'm looking for is that all-round understanding, which is what I saw in Ian Chamings. He was the whole package.

To succeed in the Den you need to have an agile mind, and you need to do the work yourself. Don't hand your business plan over to a third party, as many people do. I can spot those a mile off. I would rather see a plan that is not particularly polished but which is well thought out.

You don't need to have the skills of an accountant, but it is completely unforgivable not to have an idea of what you think your turnover is going to be. How can you expect me to invest in your business if you don't have an idea of turnover, gross and net profit, and profit before or after tax? These are fundamental numbers.

Very, very occasionally I'll come across the exception to the rule. Levi Roots with his Reggae Reggae Sauce, for example; I would not say that he had a strong grasp of numbers, but Levi is a brand in himself; it was Peter who spotted that. But what happened to Levi is extremely rare.

A good entrepreneur needs to be a reasonable risk-taker, someone who is able to consider, calculate and mitigate risk. You can't
be too much of a gambler. A successful candidate for my investment
also needs to be someone who can give straight answers to straight
questions and make me understand his or her idea. The day Ian
Chamings appeared in the Den, I had not woken up that morning
thinking, 'I want to invest in an automated DJ system.' Ian made
me understand the idea, and what's more, he made me like it. David
Pybus, who came in to present his Scents of Time company, was the
exact opposite. I could not get out of David any clear idea of why I
should invest in him. I did not invest because he could not make me
understand what the situation was with the contracts. He simply
failed to get his message across, even though I tried harder than I
would normally! But not everybody shared my problem – we
Dragons are all different. Theo and Peter both sensed a potential in
Scents of Time and (luckily for David) previous experience in this
market helped them understand what he was about. They decided
to invest. I must admit I was surprised but suspect they have a
cunning plan!

On principle, I only invest when both the product and the
would-be entrepreneur come up to my high standards. Just sometimes, though, I can see a good idea badly presented and I consider
following it up, as long as it's in an area where I'm confident I
can add real value and make a difference. When Asli Bohane
from Empty Me Picnics brought her design for a picnic bag into the
Den, for example, I thought that it was a really cute idea but her

presentation was awful. She wanted something like £40,000 and in three years I would get £10,000 return. I was thinking, 'I would get more in the bank', but I liked the picnic bag enough to make an offer. I knew exactly what I would do with that bag because I have retail experience, and I could put it into my holiday parks. I made Asli a really tough offer, but I was very clear that I wanted 51 per cent of that business because I wanted control. She couldn't accept my terms, but if she had had me on board she would have earned 49 per cent of something.

Having said that, a good idea alone is rarely enough to attract me. I get an awful lot of ideas sent through to me, but there's a big, big chasm between an idea and a business proposition. Lots of people could sit in a room for a couple of hours and come up with any number of ideas, but how many people have the ability to make their plans materialise? Very often, I'm approached with something I've heard or seen a dozen times before, and this tells me that the person has done no research. One thing that's been suggested to me over and over again is a key fob with a mobile phone which rings so that you can easily locate misplaced keys. It sounds like a very good idea, but that's all it is – an idea. So what exactly would I be investing in? It's not enough to identify a need – you have to create something physical, something real, that will provide the solution. If someone plonks a prototype for this ringing key fob down in front of me, then I might sit up and take notice.

Most of the ideas I reject are not ludicrous so much as poorly thought out. Once in a while something will come up which beggars belief, like the device for covering cats' claws to prevent them from scratching furniture. The man had this uncanny cat that would tolerate wearing these little false fingernails, but I sat there thinking, I cannot believe I am looking at this. I have cats and if I went near them to put false fingernails on they would be up the curtains.

People associate me with sales and marketing, so they're surprised when I tell them that nothing makes me more suspicious than an over-fluent sales pitch. People who are clearly salesmen and nothing else turn me off instantly. I will not invest in them, because I don't think I'm seeing the truth, I think I'm seeing what that person wants me to see, and that frightens me off, because I've got to be able to get under the skin of the person I'm talking to. I've got to be able to trust and believe in that person. People in full-on slick automatic sales mode scare the living daylights out of me.

I am more impressed by a clear, rehearsed, well-thought-out presentation than by a slick or polished one. If you're thinking of entering the Den, make your research specific and relevant. Rehearse the pitch, ideally in front of someone whose opinion you respect. Memorise your key points. Use your own language – don't try to be too clever by using 'insiders'' jargon. If you do, you'll only confuse your listener! Practise your grooming and personal presentation to make sure you feel your absolute best. Above all, be yourself. Being misleading or disingenuous is a dangerous game to play. If you're being honest, sooner or later that will show.

Between us, we Dragons achieve a good balance. For 95 per

cent of the time we can argue as much as we like when we're in the Den, then we come out and go and have lunch together and we all get on. Of course, there are moments when I think, life's too short, this isn't an argument I want to be bothered with. We're not married to each other, for heaven's sake! But we're very straight with each other. If I think somebody has invested in something silly I'll tell them so, and they'll return the compliment. If we disagree with each other on screen, nothing changes when we go out, but it's all over quite quickly. Someone will say, 'You must be mad', and then we move on.

We Dragons are a pretty fierce lot and the very nature of us is that we are highly competitive. I feel very comfortable in such a charged environment and really enjoy being in the Den where you either step up to the mark or you are out! I have a great deal of respect for the knowledge of my fellow Dragons and I appreciate the fact that being in the Den gives me access to it. If somebody knows more about a certain area than I do, it makes my investment decision much easier when I can listen to an expert asking informed questions. All of us have our own particular areas of expertise and we can all benefit from each other.

Our different skills and our contrasting personalities combined are what makes *Dragons' Den* a dynamic and successful show. We're a good team. Between us, we've got a lot of knowledge.

DEBORAH'S DRAGONS' RULES FOR SUCCESS

● **CREATE A BUSINESS PLAN** There's a big chasm between a bright idea and a viable business proposition. By building a business plan you are creating a map to your goals. Whilst it is fine to use some help in certain areas, the plan must fundamentally be yours. It must be built by you, on your visions, with your knowledge and clearly reflect your goals and milestones. Only too often I hear, I have done a business plan for the bank. Well, that is one use for it but the primary beneficiary of the plan should be those who should be following it!

● **DON'T FOOL YOURSELF** Honesty and clarity are essential in every walk of life, but for entrepreneurs they are crucial characteristics. It is easy to get carried away with a good idea: be honest with yourself. There is a difference between being passionate about your product and taking a cool, critical look at what you are planning to do with it.

● **STAY COOL UNDER PRESSURE** If you're going to enter the Den, you can't allow yourself to crumble under pressure. If you can't survive in the Den you are unlikely to be able to survive the highs and lows of the business environment.

● **RESEARCH** Know your market, know your competition and know your basic figures. Guessing or hoping on any of these is a very dangerous game to play. You need exact numbers from detailed research to show investors that you really know what you are talking about.

A LESSON IN PATENTS AND ENGINEERING:
IAN CHAMINGS AND MIXALBUM

Ian Chamings' MixAlbum has emerged triumphantly from the ordeal-by-fire that is Dragons' Den. At MixAlbum.com you can download your favourite dance tracks and mix them the way you want them at the click of a button. In other words, MixAlbum enables you to become your own DJ. Ian's experience in the Den shows how a good idea needs to be protected by patent in order for it to have value as an investment. However, even with technological expertise and the legal protection of a patent on his idea, Ian needed more than just funding. Marketing and press relations were his weakest skills, so when Deborah Meaden was the first to put in an offer he knew that her marketing background could be essential to the business succeeding.

Ian had the idea for MixAlbum while he was at university, studying for a degree in automotive engineering and DJing in his spare time. Ian has a 2:1 Masters with Honours in Automotive Engineering from the University of Bath. He graduated in 2000. His 'Eureka moment' came when he realised that he could combine the two sides of his life: 'I thought, "Hang on, I can get computers to do most of my DJing for me." And I stored it in the back of my mind.'

After graduating, Ian trained as a patent attorney. 'Our clients come to us with an invention which they need to protect in every way so they need an engineer's brain to say, 'Well, how can we get round this?' This training made it easy for Ian to get a patent together for his MixAlbum idea. The patent was granted in 2003. He received a Prince's Trust grant to develop a prototype and it then took a year to find the necessary funding. He also received a grant to convert an old barn on his parents' Devon farm into an office. This was for £40,000, from the Government's Rural Development Agency which is funded by European money. The aim of the fund is to get businesses started in specific rural areas and he qualified for this by using some of the money to build an office for MixAlbum.

Ian took his project to Business Link, the wheels were set in motion and a showcase site was launched demonstrating the software. The next stage was to get the site launched properly; to do this required more investment, more contacts, more PR – time to approach *Dragons' Den*.

Ian's background in maths and engineering enabled him to sort out the basic prototype for MixAlbum, but he also enlisted the help of Tom Hedley, now the Head Programmer at MixAlbum.com, who rewrote the code. Ian describes Tom as 'an extreme character … when we got the go-ahead he cycled down from Cheltenham with a hard drive in one of his panniers and a couple of pairs of underpants in the other, and that's how it began, down in the middle of nowhere'.

So what exactly is this invention that had to impress the Dragons? 'It's an automatic DJ. When you buy dance music, 80 per cent of it is bought in mixed compilations so one track blends seamlessly into the next. This is key for dance music, because everybody wants to listen to it mixed together, but of course, if it's already mixed together then you can't choose which tracks are mixed. My invention means that you can choose all the singles that you want then you click a button and it mixes them for you.

What made Ian apply for *Dragons' Den*?

'Everyone said, "You should be on that," and also I love watching it. I'm an avid fan. Preparing for the interview on camera was fun, even though I was quite nervous about it.'

Most of his work was market research – he had been working on the project for a while by that point and had to know the figures that he needed. Ian's advice to other entrepreneurs is that 'despite your own bias towards your idea you have to be realistic and play devil's advocate, checking every part of the plan for weaknesses. Not only so you don't look an idiot on national TV, but if it is going to be your livelihood, you need to know if it is a good idea.'

Once Ian had convinced himself that he knew the numbers, he was concerned that the cameras might make him nervous in his initial pitch, so he set up a video camera and practised over and over again. 'Watching it back was cringeworthy first of all! But it really worked, and after enough practice I was using it to see where I needed to emphasise certain points in the speech rather than just calm my nerves about the cameras being there.'

So, Ian prepared himself thoroughly: 'I knew if I got the research right, then it would be easy to go up those steps with absolute confidence.'

On the day, Ian and the other contenders were told to arrive at eight o'clock, but as with all entrepreneurs they were not told their running order. 'I was waiting right until the end. It was surreal. I thought about twenty minutes had passed and it was actually two hours. That shows you how much adrenalin was going through my system.' He took his mind off his pitch and relaxed by talking to the other inventors and he even practised further run-throughs of his presentation – but he points out, 'If it wasn't smooth by that point I don't think there would have been much hope!'

He has a vivid memory of the moment when he was standing at the bottom of the stairs:

'After the almost frantic bustling of people moving around setting up lights, getting the camera rolling and the Dragons in place, having you mic'd up, someone shouts "Action" – and there's total silence. It's very eerie walking into a room with so many people in it who are all that quiet and focused on you. I'll never forget the smell of the wooden floorboards and the sound of my steps to the pitching area before I began.'

Ian was able to deliver the piece he had memorised, but under pressure his ability to do mental arithmetic deserted him. 'Peter said, "So you expect that's a million downloads a year?" And I knew how many seconds it takes to do one mix and I know how many you can it into a year, but I'd never broken it down into weeks before, and I couldn't work it out. I thought I knew everything, but I was proved wrong. Luckily they didn't show that bit! Other than that, it all went fairly smoothly.'

Ian's impressions of the Dragons varied: he did not think his idea had attracted Duncan – apparently Duncan seemed keener to get to his supper! Ian was impressed by Richard's speed in grasping the technical side of the MixAlbum business and it was enjoyable talking to him about the patent.

'Peter didn't want his time wasted and therefore interrogated the figures, but I was able to respond and after that I think he saw the potential too, a very likeable guy ... And then there's the fantastic Deborah and Theo! Theo made sure there were a few questions in there which could have been death traps to the unready pitcher, and certainly required a bit of thought – but it's that same straight talking which keeps things focused when we're talking about the business today.'

He left the Den with two investors, Theo Paphitis and Deborah Meaden. 'While I was there I didn't really take anything in, I was just buzzing. But the crew said afterwards that you could see the Dragons' eyes light up when we were talking about the patent. I didn't just have some fancy idea; it was something that could be protected and has a technical effect. That was important.'

Ian was especially impressed by Evan Davis: 'An immensely likeable gent and one of these people who knows so much about so much! When I had the chance to chat with him for a few minutes I realised I had to go into a deeper level of information on specific parts of MixAlbum than usual – he'd obviously been paying attention!'

For Deborah Meaden, Ian was impressive right from the start. 'He was a good overall package. His training as a patent lawyer gave him a discipline. He had an extremely logical way of doing his presentation; he took us through step by step, he held his ground.' There was a potentially difficult moment near the beginning when Ian switched his device on and it didn't work. 'It wasn't actually his fault – the team had set it up and they had forgotten to switch something back on. I was watching to see whether he would fall to pieces. But he held his composure and didn't panic, and I thought, 'Now here is a guy who is cool headed, he is logical, he has identified a niche in the market and he is clearly a doer. As a combination, that for me was spot on.'

The high quality of Ian's presentation was especially important to Deborah because his product was completely out of her field. 'I and indeed all of the Dragons were looking at him as if to say what is it? How does it work? Why is it needed? So there was quite a burden on Ian's shoulders to explain it all in a way that would convince us. There was a moment when I felt, he has got everyone's attention here, he is explaining this very well – now I understand. I do not need to understand technically how it works but I understand why it is needed and I understand why it is unique.'

After committing to an investment, Deborah's practice is to go and visit the person she's taken on in their own environment. 'It tells me an awful lot,' she says. She went to visit Ian in his newly converted barn which, coincidentally, is not very far from her own home. 'I said to him, Ian, this could be a good thing or a bad thing. If the business goes wrong you are going to wish I lived a lot further away!' Ian's farmyard office 'said all the right things about him.' She was impressed that he had organised a grant for the office conversion, and created 'a very smart little office', implying that this was a serious business and that he was going to set it up properly. 'He was as impressive there as he was inside the Den. I did not feel cheated, I felt this is true, this is real.'

The next stage was the development of the website. Deborah was worried about the pace of events: 'When the programme went on air we got something like ten thousand hits in the first two hours and it actually took the website down. To me that is a nightmare because the product really should be ahead of your branding.' She told Ian that he needed a strategy to deal with potentially disappointed customers: 'I told him we have got to deal with it, otherwise we lose these customers for ever', so a data capture system was set up.

The due diligence process (where the finances of the business are checked by the investors' accountants) was carried out and in this case the procedure was quite simple because Ian's was a new company. Deborah's view is that all business issues should be debated before the investment is finalised: 'What you want to do is to agree everything, get it into the shareholders' agreement, put it together and put it to bed.' This took about a month.

Ian badly needed Deborah's advice on how to get his message

through to the music companies. 'Never underestimate the power of being involved with a Dragon,' says Deborah. 'You just get your telephone calls answered, it's as simple as that. I went through my address book, came up with some names, organised a couple of meetings, but even Ian himself found that when he phoned and said, "I'm Ian from *Dragons' Den* and I've got Theo and Deborah involved," the power of that was huge.' Ian agrees. 'The kudos, having Theo and Deborah with me, is quite literally as valuable as the money. If I had another investment of £150,000 from people who couldn't give this kudos and business acumen I don't think it would get anywhere.'

'Ian had nothing without the record companies,' continues Deborah. 'There is no point having an automated DJ system that has no records to mix so that was absolutely crucial.' Theo and Deborah went with Ian to his first meeting with Warner. 'We wanted to see Ian in that environment, see how he got on in a meeting. But our presence also meant that we were talking to the right person, the person who could make the decision.'

Deborah's PR skills were vitally important to Ian. 'I'm a patent attorney geek, an engineering geek – my PR skills are zero. So Deborah taught me an awful lot.' Branding was also a problem. 'With branding,' says Deborah, 'the point is that everybody should instantly know what the product is or at least they should be given a taste or an expectation of it. What Ian had done to date looked slightly cobbled together. I made him see the importance of it; I pointed out that he had a lot of competitors, particularly on the internet. I said, 'You have to hit people in the face with exactly what this is.' I think my putting emphasis on it meant that branding came right to the top of the list. And the great thing about Ian is, you agree a plan of action and before you know it he has got a lot of people who could do the branding, plus reasons why he thinks they are the right people.'

Theo and Deborah soon realised, having watched Ian in meetings, that they could trust him to function successfully independently of them. 'What we tend to do now is have a chat before the meetings, decide what the agenda is, make sure what the strategy is, and then leave Ian to get on with it.'

The Dragons were able to give Ian a realistic sense of time scales. 'Ian thought it was all going to happen tomorrow, as everybody does. We are where Theo and I thought we would be, which is probably slightly behind the pace as far as Ian is concerned. But when we were advising on our shareholders' agreement we actually advised Ian to cut himself some slack on his business plan. In other words we said to him, Look, if you're running, say, two months behind your business plan we will be OK with it as long as we understand why.'

Ian admits that getting the music has taken longer than he thought it would, but now deals have been signed with Sony, Warner and EMI. 'We have captured 80 per cent of the dance market!' Deborah enthuses. The Ministry of Sound wanted to organise a launch party: 'They'll be launching their website and our website; we've licensed our stuff to them and we get a fee for that, and we're selling their tracks on our website and they get a fee for that, and that is fantastic,' Ian explains. He is delighted to find that he is already getting a great many returning customers: 'So many of our customers are repeat customers so it must mean that what we are doing is right. What we've got to do now is make sure we get enough content on.'

At MixAlbum, the customer is not charged anything for the mixing. 'You can buy the singles that you want at 99p and in a good quality format and for that we will store them. Whenever you want them mixed, whichever tracks, you choose the ones you want from your library and push "go" and it downloads it.' Recently a speed change function has been added: 'That's great because people who want to do workouts and spinning classes and things like that can choose their beats per minute. We've had a lot of e-mails about that, from aerobics instructors, people saying this is just fantastic for our classes.'

Ian's deal with the Dragons is to let them have 40 per cent of the company for £150,000. He regards this as a bargain. The money, the marketing, PR and negotiation skills, the strong personalities and the power of TV fame have all made a dramatic difference. 'We had the technology,' says Ian, 'but we had no footing in the music industry – we were a nobody to them.' The roar of the Dragons has made the music industry sit up and take notice. 'It's very exciting; it's all being done from a cowshed in the middle of nowhere. There's a farmyard behind us, there's a view of rolling green fields and Dartmoor 38 miles in the distance in front of us, and it's just ideal.'

Ian's excitement is, he feels, shared by the Dragons. 'They've been incredibly helpful, and you can tell they are enjoying this project – I am absolutely sure of it.' Deborah certainly seems confident that her investment will pay off: 'I cannot emphasise enough that, to me, Ian is a perfect investment. That is, somebody who seeks advice, does not expect me to run their business for them, and, to be honest, knows most of the answers himself. So often I've said to Ian, "Well, what do *you* think?" and he has been right. I think MixAlbum is great – one of my favourites of the ideas to emerge from the Den.'

A LESSON IN EXCLUSIVE LICENSING DEALS:
KC JONES AND KLENZ

KC Jones arrived at the Den looking for investment in his self-contained sanitising unit, which he'd christened 'Klenz'. He was keen to show its unique properties – chemical-free, the unit doesn't use water or sterilising fluid to achieve 99.8 per cent sanitisation of bacteria and viruses. He brought with him a pair of smelly trainers to demonstrate how the deodoriser works. His experience in the Den was positive, but afterwards the Dragon investment fell away, showing how exclusive licensing agreements are crucial to investors. KC's story ends happily – his time in the Den brought in new investment and his business is thriving.

KC Jones is an ex-fire officer from Staffordshire. After retiring from the Fire Service in 2000 he developed a second career as an entrepreneur. 'My theory is that everybody knows somebody who has come up with an idea for a new product, but not many people get it off the ground. I help these inventions become reality.'

KC's involvement ranges from getting technical drawings or card models done, to getting prototypes made, to finding retail outlets and giving advice on marketing. He compares himself to a coal miner : 'In every ton of coal I will find a diamond.'

The invention KC chose to show the Dragons is a cleanse machine: 'It's like a microwave oven. It was introduced to me as a machine that makes shoes stop smelling. When I started doing a little research into how it worked I realised that it had far more potential than that.' He chose the Klenz because he had 100 per cent exclusivity to it.

KC was looking for an investment of £100,000 in return for 30 per cent of his business. He demonstrated the machine to the Dragons using a pair of smelly shoes and a lump of blue cheese: one blast from the machine and the odour disappeared. He explained that the machine achieved 99.8 per cent sanitisation without the use of chemicals, water or sterilising fluid.

The technology was very advanced – it had been developed for use in spacecraft and was called 'nanosilver' technology. 'The technology was well known but not particularly well used.' The machines are manufactured in Korea. KC took one along to a chiropodist and found that foot problems such as verrucas are hard to eliminate because spores live in shoes and socks, causing recontamination. 'The chiropodist said this would be a great thing for their patients; they could sanitise their footwear whilst having their feet treated. So we quickly saw a potential market there and started selling it direct to chiropodists.'

When KC demonstrated the machine to the Dragons, he had already sold 200 machines in four months. He bought each machine for £89 and sold it for £299 plus VAT. He believed that, as well as chiropodists and podiatrists, gyms and health clubs would be receptive to the idea. Instead of stuffing a pair of sweaty trainers into a bag where they would fester, customers could pop them into a Klenz machine at the gym and take them home odour-free.

He also wanted to tackle the domestic market. He told the Dragons that the machines had dozens of uses in the home – for sanitising babies' bottles, or cutlery, or electrical equipment. The Dragons were divided as to how useful they personally would find this machine. Richard felt that people were too paranoid about germs as it was, and that a little exposure to bacteria built up natural immunities. Theo, on the other hand, was quite impressed, and said he would want one in his own home.

Theo was, however, less impressed by KC's reply when he asked whether the machine was covered by patents. Theo was worried that it would be easily copied, and KC had to admit that he was on shaky ground. Theo pointed out that KC was really only an agent; the Klenz was not his own product. He felt sure that, as the technology had been around for some time, it would quickly be reproduced, and the market would be flooded.

Deborah was also worried about this. She felt that, while KC might have cornered a particular market, there would soon be lots of people coming in and doing something similar. KC, however, was confident that he could reach the finishing post before his competitors had taken off.

Richard was not convinced that there was a significant household market, but he was interested in the fact that KC felt he had not yet 'touched the sides' in terms of chiropodists and gym clubs. To the surprise of the other Dragons, Richard offered £50,000 in exchange for 25 per cent of the business, but he stated that a condition of his investment would be a guarantee that there was no UK competitor for this technology.

Deborah had almost made up her mind not to invest. She was not sure that KC was the sort of person she could do business with. 'I have met the KCs of this world and they are fantastic. They're full of enthusiasm, they are eternal optimists but it is very, very difficult to keep them focused.' Watching KC in the Den, she was telling herself that this was neither the type of person nor the type of product she usually invested in, and, like the other Dragons, she felt that the product was insufficiently protected. But at the same time she told herself that she could be wrong; after all, the Klenz was already selling strongly.

'Without a protective patent and a protected licence, the business was worth basically nothing,' she explained. 'It came from Korea, which suggested that it would be easy to copy, and there's no point in having a good product when everybody else can get their hands on it and perhaps sell it better than we can.'

It was Richard's attitude that made her mind up. 'I was about to go out when Richard leapt in and said, "Deborah, before you declare your hand…" Now, Richard is very hot on licensing and patents, so I thought, if he's prepared to take the chance, then so should I. I think I was investing as much in the co-investor as I was in KC. If you respect someone's judgement, then you have to take that into account. Also, it wasn't an awful lot of money. So I thought, well, this is worth a punt.'

Deborah declared her hand. She believed there was a finite end to the product: 'I would invest because it would allow me to get a return on my interest in that period of time. I don't have to worry about what's going to happen five years on.' Like Richard, she offered KC £50,000 for 25 per cent of the business.

This was a change from the 30 per cent originally on offer. 'It's a huge chunk,' KC pointed out, and tried to get the Dragons to agree to 40 per cent, but they stood firm, because, as Deborah put it, 'There are huge risks to this product becoming, not obsolete, but just flooded. It's got to happen quickly and I think with us on board it will happen quickly.' KC decided that the chance to work along-side the Dragons was worth the sacrifice, and the deal was made.

As mentioned earlier, Deborah's practice is always to visit the person in whom she has invested in their own environment, so she soon set off for Birmingham to inspect KC's offices. This happened too quickly for KC's liking: 'It was unfortunate because Dragons want to do things at their pace and I had a different agenda alto-gether.' Deborah was taken aback by what she found. 'He had a very nice little set of offices and some very good people around him, but I also discovered complications, because he had lots of other businesses which were integrated into this initial business and I could just imagine the time it was going to take to sort it all out.'

KC had been hoping to interest Deborah in his other projects: 'The Klenz is not important to me as a product, it's not my baby. I know it has got a shelf-life of one or two years which all of the Dragons identified and I agreed. When Deborah came here I said look, I've got all these other things here that we can be involved in, but she immediately stood back and said no, I'm investing in just this one product. That was a setback to me as I know I can sell this product anyway.'

Deborah and KC agreed to set up a new company, to separate the sanitiser from his other projects, but other problems were arising. Deborah said, 'I was getting a lot of e-mails saying, "Be careful, these are not sterilisers, they are sanitisers."' As she would when becoming involved with any business, she had sent KC a questionnaire: 'It's three pages of basic questions – who owns the company, what is its registered number, technical data, basic stuff. There are about 30 questions, and when I get the answers back two or three of them always give me a certain feeling, a sense that there may be a problem in this area and I home in on it. In KC's case, I started focusing very heavily on three things: health and safety; the exclusivity agreement with the Koreans to bring it into the UK; and patent right.

Alarm bells were beginning to ring. Deborah asked KC for verification of numbers for the goods he'd already sold, but he was unable or unwilling to provide these. Deborah had a feeling that the deal was not going to come to fruition: 'You just think, I do not like the silence.'

After three weeks, she received an e-mail from KC saying that he did not think he would be able to satisfy her and Richard on the patent and its exclusivity arrangements. He also said that, with all his other projects on the go he was not going to be able to give this one the time and attention that the Dragons would require. By this stage, Deborah was not surprised to find that the deal had collapsed. There had just been too many complications.

For his part, KC was disappointed not to be working with Deborah. 'I think I struck a chord with Deborah. I saw beyond the Dragon veneer and I felt a warmth, I really felt I'd be able to work well with her. I think she liked me too, she liked my enthusiasm and motivation. I had hoped we would have a long future together. But whereas I hoped she'd see the overall picture as I see it, she just wanted to focus on the one product.'

However, the story has a happy ending. 'I had another investor contact me – David Lloyd, who owns a chain of health clubs, had seen it on the television. He said, "I'm interested in you and in your business as a whole." He offered to match their money.'

Despite the collapse of the initial deal, KC says that going into the Dragons' Den was the best thing he ever did. 'Going into the Den was a calculated risk because I thought if I do go in there and get spat out, that could be potentially damaging, but as it turned out it was a fantastic help. Since then I have been inundated with new inventions, and with people who want to invest in new products. It's incredible, but from just 15 minutes on the television I still get people recognising me when I'm out shopping. And of course that's how I got my new investor, David Lloyd. So, yes, it was a wonderful experience and I would recommend it to anybody.'

THEO PAPHITIS

Theo Paphitis was originally invited to join Dragons' Den *for the second series, shown on BBC2 in 2005. At first he had doubts but soon settled in to bring his own wit and style to the programme. Here he reflects on the show and the fledgling entrepreneurs that came under his searching gaze. He considers what makes him want to invest – and how the Den has affected his own life and career.*

I started doing media interviews when I took over Millwall Football Club. Frankly, I was crap at it. You see yourself on the box and it is weird. Your perception of yourself – how you look, how you articulate – is totally different to the reality. It takes a while just to get used to your own oddities. For example, I did a programme for BBC2 called *Back to the Floor*. It came out okay, everyone loved it but I so disliked myself in it I decided I wasn't going to do any more TV after that.

Then, many years later, after I resigned from Millwall, I got a phone call from the BBC asking if I would be interested in appearing on this show called *Dragons' Den* which had already run one series. But I told them, I'm not very photogenic and I never really learned to talk properly so it's going to be rather difficult to be on BBC2 which is very lah-di-dah and highbrow. They kept on asking me to go to an audition and I didn't go.

Finally, they came back and said, 'Look, we have done all the interviews with the other possible Dragons and we are still not happy. Please come and do an audition.' But I couldn't see the point. My argument was that they must have seen the stuff I had done, so what was the point of going and sitting in a chair looking gormless for them? But I did ultimately agree to go and have a cup of tea with them. I popped into Television Centre and the devious so-and-sos had an entrepreneur there ready and waiting to pitch to me. And he was fantastic! It was a company called Earworms which has been hugely successful doing language-learning to music CDs. I think you can even download them from iTunes now. They are smashing people and it was a really good pitch. I explained to them that though I thought the business would be successful, they actually couldn't justify the need for investment. But I really enjoyed it.

At the end of the meeting, the BBC guys said they'd get back to me but I wasn't having that. After all, they had been pretty cheeky in the way they had got me to audition, so I gave them ten minutes to decide. They came back within five minutes and that was that.

The first time I was in the Den, I was nervous as a kitten. Everyone else was experienced, they had done lots of television, they had a history together. I was the outsider coming in. The only person I had met before was the great Peter Jones and we had some affinity which helped. On the other hand, I felt there was a general friction with Rachel Elnaugh – she seemed spiky, a bit prickly in that series – perhaps because it turned out that all was not perfect with her own businesses at the time.

I was surprised too at how small the location was – it was in this grotty warehouse, so dusty and dirty it was ridiculous. Plus it was baking hot with lights, four or five cameras, sound people, floor manager, runners, make-up girl and so on. At that stage, we weren't even allowed out and the food they brought in was appalling; I reckon convicts get better food. Above all, everyone was so serious. After the first day, I wondered what the hell I had let myself in for. I was bored stiff and in a grim situation: four weeks of my life stuck in this environment yawned before me. *Dragons' Den* series one had been very much like bank managers and accountants proffering their wisdom. That was the atmosphere and I couldn't take it. So I began stepping up the jokes, the light-heartedness. I said things on air which the other Dragons assured me would get nowhere near the final edit but to everyone's surprise they started appearing in the programme and even featuring in the trailers.

It started almost by accident. There was one guy who came up to pitch to us who really annoyed me. He refused to listen, he was condescending and patronising, and I have to admit I lost it. I said,

'Listen, mate, I would rather stick pins in my eyes than invest in your business.' There was a gasp – this was not something that you heard on *Dragons' Den*. It was not very 'bank manager' – but it worked, people liked it and gradually the others started to use some of the same style. That was part and parcel, I believe, of the programme's growth. It became more mainstream, it relaxed. I was quoted as telling so-called entrepreneurs, 'The wheel's going round but the hamster died a long time ago,' 'The lights are on but no one's home' and 'I would rather pass a kidney stone than invest in you.' That one got a load of letters from 'Furious of Tunbridge Wells' saying I was not respecting the painful experience of having kidney stones! But suddenly *Dragons' Den* became fun, we were talking like real people. There was even a rebellion about the food. We insisted on going out, though we would invariably get back early and sober. So the production team relaxed as well and the camaraderie grew all round.

I thoroughly enjoyed the following series. The whole chemistry was different. All five Dragons were prepared to invest and be competitive: you could feel the sparks fly.

But what about the people who step up in front of us, who come to pitch their products and ideas? Imagine the nerves you feel, being under the lights, just a few minutes to convince us, waiting for us to decide on something that you are passionate about, deliver a judgement that will affect your whole future. It must be absolutely horrendous. Unfortunately, it is not my job to make anyone feel at ease. My job is to analyse the pitch and the vibes you give out. We have no idea who is about to appear in front of us or what they will propose but, in all honesty, I would say that 95 per cent of the time, I have made my mind up within the first minute.

Why? For a start, I never cease to be astonished by the number of people who turn up and fail to tick the basic boxes. Everyone who comes to pitch to us knows they will have to answer questions about their business. Supposedly they know it inside-out because they are living it every day. But viewers are always asking me questions like, 'What was that idiot doing on your show without knowing how to run through their numbers?' I'm here to tell you this doesn't just happen in the Den. It happens in business constantly. Yet the answer is blindingly obvious: preparation. Do your homework and know your business and there is nothing that will come up that you won't be able to answer with style.

Secondly, you have to be realistic. In the Dragons' Den, we look for the same good return on our investment as any other investor. We do not want to run your business for you. We do not intend to engage in a lifelong, deep and meaningful relationship – though, should your business start showing signs of serious potential, we will probably want to go on investing for as long as it takes to turn potential into success. But if we do invest, we intend to support you and be your sounding board as long as it takes and as long as we continue to have faith in you.

I am also often grabbed by people in the street asking why I didn't invest in a project they thought was a fabulous scheme. I explain that the idea was good but that it could not be translated into a moneymaking venture. This goes back to my unconquerable belief that in business we're in regular danger of making ourselves into 'busy fools'. We take on a project, devote time and resources to it even though we may know in our hearts that the outcome of it is never going to be financial success.

So what makes a successful entrepreneur? That's tough because it is not a simple question of six ounces of this, four ounces of that in set proportions. Hunger, drive, ambition, dreams plus the will to actually make it happen, you need all those. And you have to find a way to keep up your confidence. One of the first lessons you need to absorb before appearing on *Dragons' Den* or in front of any potential investor is how to conquer your inevitable fears. Yes, standing there with the glare of the lights in your face and the cameras rolling can be scary, but it should not really be any more unsettling than when you go and plead with the bank manager in his swank office. Either way, you have to acknowledge the anxiety within you – and then just get on with it.

One of the facets of *Dragons' Den* I have grown to love is its unpredictability. You sit there and you have had six, seven, eight projects in front of you and they have all been rubbish. You have been there since early morning, it is now the end of the afternoon and it is baking hot; you long to fall asleep. You think to yourself, 'I don't need to do this, why am I doing it?' Then your answer comes. Just when you lose the will to live, 'Bang!' – in comes something that really tickles and excites you. It may be the pitch, it may be the person who gets to you first. It may even be both at the same time – people like Christian Lane with Foldio – and suddenly, they pierce the heat and the frustration and you think, 'My God, this person really is worth backing.'

None of the Dragons are omniscient. None of us would ever guarantee someone is going to be a success; it just wouldn't happen. However, what you do come to see very quickly is whether a person has a good proposal and, with a bit of guidance, could go somewhere. For me, that is fantastic. I've made plenty of money, I don't get out of bed every morning because I need to go and make money. I deal with all my various investments in the same way: I do things because I want to do them, they give me a buzz. At the end of the year, money is a by-product and a measure of how successful I have been in that year. But seriously, if money and money alone was the reason I had to get out of bed, I would go to bed and spend my whole life there. So when I invest in somebody on *Dragons' Den*, I am not doing it just to make money there either. It is because it is exciting, it catches my interest, it has all the advantages I want or otherwise I ain't going to do it. And is it the person who makes it exciting or is it the product? Silly question. It has to be both.

We now come to the so-called celebrity factor, the golden touch of television that turns toads into stars overnight. I can tell you straight, fame certainly hasn't changed my life. Money has, fame hasn't. You can do whatever you want to do with money, it brings all sorts of comfort and privileges. It also brings its complications because when you are seen to be an incredibly wealthy person you find there are an awful lot of people who expect things of you, looking for unrealistic generosity, and suddenly whatever you do is never enough. I try to deal with it by walking around in my jeans. I stroll down Wimbledon High Street outside the office and people look at me and get used to me and realise I am actually quite normal.

The best thing that has come from the Den has been the *type* of fame. I was recognised in the street quite often before the Den because I did a lot of stuff on TV about football and the Football League and Football Association, but I get a different sort of recognition now. It is much nicer, people just want to talk to you and most of them have got an idea they are bursting to try out. As long as you are pleasant, I have always found people are remarkably decent and polite in return. What does amuse me is the shock they seem to get when they see me on the way to Spain on an ordinary, basic airline with my kids. There I am with the kids running riot and I'm chasing them up and down the aircraft just like any dad. People are almost disappointed – they expect me to be on a private jet, jetting off somewhere – but eventually, towards the end of the flight, they build up courage and someone comes up to enquire why I'm on this particular plane. So I tell them: how am I going to get me and all my kids to Spain at reasonable speed? I suppose I could walk but that seems like a rotten idea. Private jet? No, I have got a family, I lead a family life and do a lot of the ordinary things that everybody does.

So that's the story of me and the Den. I have met some great people through doing it and no doubt will meet plenty more – plus a few idiots besides! Do I have any disappointments or regrets about the programme? Perhaps one. In spite of my impressive national television profile, my business colleagues still treat me in the same casual manner as they have always done. No change there whatsoever!

When the Den is over, it's always back to the day job and, apart from the fledgling new entrepreneurs I'm looking forward to mentoring, it really hasn't changed very much. Time to get on and see what fresh opportunities tomorrow may bring.

THEO PAPHITIS' DRAGONS' RULES FOR SUCCESS

● **CASH IS ALL** A lack of profit is like a cancer, it will kill you slowly but a lack of cash flow is like a fatal heart attack, you're dead. Make sure you have enough cash to trade. Even if you are making a profit, if you don't have enough cash flow to support your turnover you need to make appropriate financial arrangements.

● **WORK OUT THE WHAT-IFS** Work out your business in absolute detail. If you've got the what-ifs buttoned down (because they will happen) you'll be able to convince people to support you.

● **COMMON SENSE IS NOT COMMON** My guiding principle: 'KISS' – 'Keep It Simple, Stupid'. Simple communication means everybody buys into what you're trying to achieve – including staff, financiers, suppliers and customers.

● **DON'T SCRIMP ON THE TECHNOLOGY** Be sensible with your systems, but don't scrimp on them. If you're going to ask people to support you, you need the right information available on a regular basis so you can share it with everyone involved.

● **DON'T LET THINGS STAGNATE** You've got to be constantly looking at how to be ahead of the game. Put in new initiatives, set new targets each year. That way your staff will get more experience and the business stays fresh and moves faster. Do not assume anything.

A LESSON IN CREATING THE PERFECT PITCH:
GAVIN WHEELDON'S APPLIED LANGUAGE SOLUTIONS

Gavin Wheeldon may be 'the one that got away' – a rare example of a great investment opportunity that escaped the Dragons. Based in Manchester and with a background in sales and IT, Gavin had spotted a gap in the market. He set up a web-based business to transform translation from a cottage industry to a wide-based professional service. By the time he arrived at the Den, Gavin had won a National Business Award and 'North East Entrepreneur of the Year'. With big ambitions for his company, he was looking for an extra injection of cash from the Dragons. Gavin thought he knew his business through and through and decided to take a hardball approach to negotiation. It was a tactic that may have deterred the Dragons from a profitable investment and lost Gavin the profile and expertise of the top table.

Even the most seasoned salesmen get nervous. Gavin Wheeldon has been in business since he was 12. Then, he was running a schoolboy gardening and window-cleaning concern. In his teens, he was thrown out of college – the staff said he was making too much money selling kitchens to concentrate on his studies. He has built at least two companies up from nothing to major growth. However, as he mounted the stairs to the Dragons' Den, Gavin felt as if he had swallowed the Sahara. He tried to reassure himself as he had so many times before a big sale. 'There's nothing they can ask me where I can't give an instant answer. I've proven results, I am passionate about what I do and that's bound to be contagious.'

But Gavin had to admit he was shaky. He was about to face real business expertise, five entrepreneurs skilled at peeling away any salesman's glossy veneer to get to the hard facts beneath.

'Hi. I'm Gavin Wheeldon, Managing Director of translations company Applied Language Solutions. At the top end we do websites for Nike and Robbie Williams but if you wanted to get "I love my Mum" tattooed across your back in Hebrew, then applied-language.com could get that done too. We've been going for three years now and are set to do a £3.2 million turnover this year. We want to get to floatation within five years so I'm here today to ask for £250,000 for 4 per cent equity.'

There was a pause in the Den as the Dragons assessed Gavin's pitch. Richard Farleigh was the first cool voice asking: 'Did you say £250,000 for 4 per cent? I think that's the lowest percentage offer I've ever seen in the Dragons' Den.'

A ripple of agreement went round. Gavin held his nerve. He had always been keen to work with Richard, admired his knowledge of technology and thought the two of them would be a great fit. If he could persuade Richard to invest or even just be on his board the value would be immense. Richard leaned back and penetrated deeper into the business with a question. 'What's this free service on the web?'

Gavin had a clear reply: 'Instant on-line translation. It's about 70 per cent accurate, a gimmick to attract visitors. It acts as the driver, the revenue is all from professional, human translation.'

But Richard had more to investigate: 'What's your profit on your £3.2 million in revenue?'

Gavin knew this was the key to the investment. 'If we continue on track for what we're doing at the moment we will hit just over £400,000 net profit for the year.'

'That's good,' said Richard. Richard's tone had changed; he was impressed and rightly so – in his career so far, Gavin has made remarkable progress and shown a great deal of resilience.

'I started a business when I was 19, ended up with 50 staff, but I was over-traded, didn't understand the fundamentals of business and went under. I've always been of the belief that if things go wrong you pick yourself up and try again. So I learnt some stark lessons and went into IT sales.' Gavin built up to selling heavy-weight Oracle systems and was poached to work for a language company. One of the elements was translation.

'I looked at the market and it was very small, very niche. Nobody really understood technology or business. Everybody was coming at it from an academic level, "translation agencies" were guaranteed to be just one or two people. And it's wonderful to be academic and fluffy but let's be ruthless, let the business be profit driven.'

When the company he was working for said they were not inter-ested, Gavin left. He had nothing but his final salary cheque and the hope of some quick sales.

'I walked up the few stairs to the back bedroom on a Monday morning and I was officially in business. I was excited, over-whelmed, anxious. I sat at the computer, started picking up the phone and asking who bought translation. Then I just searched out linguists. It was a bit haphazard because I had no language skills and couldn't check the work and at first we did have some furious customers. In the end I'd run up £57,000 worth of credit card debt and re-mortgaged the house for 30 grand. I decided to take another gamble. I rented my first office space and hired a Project Manager so that I could concentrate on the selling while they concentrated on the delivery.'

Like so many start-ups, the business demanded endless hours. In the day, Gavin worked on leads, while at night he returned to his computer.

'I was doing a lot of search engine marketing to try and get incoming leads. Nobody in that industry had dreamed of doing it properly so we started to climb very quickly up the search rankings. I did a lot of research on word density and how you to get your site to rank better – build pages, write articles, anything to get more incoming traffic to the site.'

Three years later, Gavin had 70 staff with 7,000 freelance trans-lators. He had ranking systems for every translator based on every job he has ever done. The business was scientific and slick. Gavin's optimism was high – perhaps too high. The deal he offered the Dragons valued his business at £6,000,000. Theo Paphitis wanted to know why. So Gavin told him: 'I've worked on a "profits to earnings" ratio of 15 and I've done that within the industry.' Theo interjected, 'Fifteen of what?' Gavin told him, 'The projected net profit of this year.'

But Theo knows his numbers: 'So it's 15 times a figure that you might achieve, which is about £300,000?' 'About £400,000,' said Gavin, and then Theo closed in with his killer comment: 'Profits to earnings are calculated after deduction of tax.'

Gavin had to admit he was wrong: 'Well, I've learnt something.' And Theo was on to him: 'You come and ask me to invest £250,000 and you want me to teach you at the same time?'

A chill went through the Den. Gavin knew he had made a mistake. Theo was right: in valuing his company, Gavin used predicted rather than actual profits and over-estimated those profits by not making deductions for tax. Duncan Bannatyne looked to capitalise on the error. 'Gavin, you just learned your valuation isn't as good as you thought. So with that in mind are you going to change the amount of equity you're offering?'

Before the show, Gavin had set himself a personal limit: he would offer up to 10 per cent of the equity, but now he found himself wondering whether that was right. 'It's a well-established business, we're achieving 300–400 per cent growth year on year and that is invaluable. There's no mights, it's an £11 billion industry with an 11 per cent annual growth rate and we're storming it.'

Gavin decided to hold firm at his original offer: £250,000 for only 4 per cent of equity. Peter Jones immediately declared himself out; Theo Paphitis quickly followed. Duncan Bannatyne came back with a counter proposal: 'I would be interested in investing. It's very risky – so I wouldn't invest all the money, I'd invest £125,000. But for that I'd want 9 per cent of your company.'

Gavin had an offer to invest but it was only half of the money. He was excited and keen to hook Duncan. However, he was in a tricky place. Under the rules of *Dragons' Den*, he had to get an offer of all of the money. Ideally, Deborah Meaden or Richard Farleigh would agree to invest the other half. Otherwise Gavin could leave empty-handed. Deborah wanted him to accept the fact that he got his valuation wrong. She said: 'The equity level is just not going to excite me. I might as well state now: I'm out.'

It was another blow for Gavin. Once again, the valuation, the basic flaw so mercilessly drilled out by Theo, had become Gavin's Achilles' heel. Only Richard Farleigh remained to partner Duncan Bannatyne for the full investment, but Richard was all too clear about his position. 'This business is a "copycat" business. The reason it's done well is that you are so good. It's not the sector you're in, it may not even be the product. It's the way you've run it and you're fantastic at that. If you were in a new and emerging market I would back you, but in this sector – it's a super-competitive sector and I don't want to do it. Your valuation I can't even talk about because it's completely flawed. I'm going to step out.'

Everyone but Duncan was out now. Gavin was left with one last slim possibility. Would Duncan Bannatyne save the day by increasing his offer? He had asked for 9 per cent of the equity and Gavin was happy to accept that if only Duncan would invest the full amount. Duncan considered and finally shook his head saying, 'Gavin, I think you'll probably prove all the Dragons wrong – even me. And I think you'll do tremendously well. Best of luck.'

Gavin left the Dragons' Den that day with nothing. If it had only been a matter of the equity he was offering, he might have won the Dragons over. But Theo Paphitis' forensic dissection of his valuation introduced a note of scepticism that Gavin could not quell. Today, Gavin is unrepentant.

'I like the guy. I respect what he's done, but I know the growth potential in the business. If you take the scientific formula it would come out at less, but you have to take the intangibles into account, look at the proven growth model that we've achieved. The only thing I might have done in hindsight is got an external company to value the business. If I'd asked our accountant to do me a valuation and put it on letter-headed paper then I could say, "Well, that is a true valuation from an accountant."'

And, in spite of his failure, *Dragons' Den* was a terrific experience for him. 'I was elated. It was good fun. Once I got into the questions, the sort of sparring, you might call it, it was fantastic. We certainly got some incoming enquiries after the show went out which was good. Also, I think it's helped open doors and build rapport with people.'

Since then, as always, Gavin has picked himself up and kept going. And his business has kept going with him, growing from strength to strength.

'We are forecasting next year a nearly 300 per cent growth on our current turnover. We do 150 languages so pretty much any commercial language, plus a lot of our processes are automated so our Project Managers can manage very big volumes because they're only doing the high-level tasks. We've got six or seven offices world-wide now and we've won a contract very recently for £3 million with a big international company. We've just been asked to tender for work which is $7 million a year, and there's a good chance we'll win that. We've got so many things lined up that if we only win 10 per cent of what we've got out there we'll be flying.'

And what about the fatal flaws in his valuation? Has Theo been proved right? Not according to Gavin. 'We've had a number of approaches with venture capitalists that value our company at £10 million at least, never mind the 6 that I valued it at for the show. We actually did entertain one venture capital company and went through the process. We decided, even though the offer was fantastic – £2 million for between 15 and 20 per cent – we can manage some more growth organically before we need to take any major investment.'

It seems that Gavin Wheeldon may be the one that got away. Yet, secretly, he still has hopes of one of the Dragons.

'After the show, as I got to the top of the stairs, Duncan said to me, "Gavin, if you want a non-executive chairman, let me know." I asked, "How much will that cost me?" and he said, "Nothing, I'll do it for free." For me, the whole point of going on there was to get somebody on the board and now it looked like I had got some-one excellent! I really admire Duncan for what he has done, I've followed it up since and am hoping at some point I'll get him tied down. To have Duncan, even as a mentor, that would be amazing!'

Gavin has had a career of radical highs and lows. At the moment, everything seems set fair for success, but what if, by some misfortune, the Dragons' uncertainty about Applied Language Solutions eventually proves right? What has Gavin learned from his experience as an entrepreneur?

'The first thing I'd say if somebody is thinking of starting a business is "stop thinking and start doing". If you fail you try again. The worst thing you can ever do is not do it. I failed one business because I didn't have proper financial controls in, so make sure that cashflow forecasting is done again and again.

'Also, about a year and a half into the business, I took time out to do proper strategy planning. A lot of companies say, "We're too busy, I just need to worry about this month's sales." I took what was then a very small management team offsite for two days and we looked at where we were and where we wanted to be. We put together a mission, vision and values. We examined critical success factors and what actions were needed. It's the best thing I have ever done because it makes the entire business pull in the same direction. There is no doubt from anybody in our company now where this business is going on a monthly, quarterly and annual basis.'

He looks back on his appearance before the Dragons with equal enthusiasm.

'One thing that's changed is when I saw myself I realised how much weight I'd put on. I've been on a proper diet since. Apart from that, I still know where I'm going, I've got the same determined focus, but, you know what? I definitely want to get into one of those chairs. Next time I'm in the Dragons' Den, I'm going to be on the other side.'

And what does the Dragon think who pulled him to bits? It was Theo Paphitis who really rattled Gavin. How does Theo view their encounter then and everything that's happened since? The answer comes with a characteristic shrug:

'People might say, "He did *Dragons' Den* and the Dragons turned him down. Now look – he is doing so well!" but they don't understand. Often, in cases like these, we didn't turn down the business, we just turned down the investment.

'You see, the fact I do not invest in something does not necessarily make it a bad business. It is just not right for me. If someone comes to me and values his business at a full price and for my investment I end up with a small minority holding, I am not going to do it. Gavin offered me a tiny stake. Why am I going to spend any mental time on that? Where is my upside? It is simply not exciting enough.

'I said to him at the time that he didn't need the money and I was proven right there. I don't really know what he was there for from us. If the business has grown, that's fine. Good luck to you, Gavin.'

A LESSON IN HOLDING A PATENT:
CHRISTIAN LANE'S FOLDIO

Christian Lane from Surrey was only 19 when he stepped up in front of the Dragons. Christian had studied graphic design at A Level and had found himself lugging around huge folders to carry his artwork. Then he had an inspiration – an innovative product called Foldio, which halved the size of these ungainly folders without creasing the paper. As he came forward to make his pitch, it was the climax of nearly three years of relentless spadework for a young man who had fired up his business career when most teenagers have barely got their heads around GCSEs. Christian is a living lesson in getting every aspect of an original product not just prepared and ready to go but secured by proper patent as well.

Few people would have known it, but Christian Lane has always had a phobia about speaking in front of an audience. It was not until a few months earlier, when he turned 18, that he was finally old enough to form a limited company. He had the retailers on standby, costings, tooling and the product line ready, even prototypes manufactured. Everything was ready to go: he was just waiting for an injection of investment to get it out to retail outlets in the UK.

Then he'd hit a roadblock: his age. He went for meetings at the bank. They would not finance an 18-year-old. He looked everywhere to get money but no one would back someone so young. Frantic, he scanned the net for ideas. Nothing. Then, as dawn was breaking one morning after a long night's work, an advertisement came up on Christian's screen: apply for *Dragons' Den*. It was his last hope.

Within weeks, he was in the Den. Five minutes before he went on, it hit him that he was actually going to have to prove himself. He was astonished to hear his own voice come out of his mouth.

'My name's Christian and I'm looking for an £80,000 investment for a 15 per cent stake in my company. My new product, Foldio, reduces the size of paper by 50 per cent leaving it perfectly flat. There is also a professional range used by designers and architects. I've had interest from two major retailers: WH Smith and Staples have both said they are willing to place an order. I'm looking for an investment to develop, manufacture and market so this product can really achieve its demand.'

In spite of his anxiety, Christian projected confidence, but Peter Jones needed reassurance on the real potential of Foldio. 'Christian, I really, really like the product. Have you done projections for this? Year one. What do you expect to do?'

Christian replied: 'Year one turnover, £450,000. Profit for year one, £225,000. My time is completely dedicated to this. This is my passion. I've invested £10,000 of my own money so far just for product development.'

Peter asked how he had done this and Christian said he had raised funds from his last company which dealt in a little bit of import/export from mainland China. Peter said: 'Christian, you're talking like a 30-year-old – you're 19!'

It was hardly surprising Peter Jones was impressed. Like many young entrepreneurs, Christian's first idea had come from the internet. Importing innovative media devices such as MP3 and MP4 players had given him the seed money for his big idea.

'I was 15 when I looked on eBay and saw there was potential if I bought these media devices in batches and sold them individually. Then I realised that if I ordered greater quantities there was more profit to be made, so I started up my own website. I had a number of brands and sold directly to the public. I did that for probably about a year. I decided I would save up the money I made to invest in the next opportunity. I didn't really realise that it would be in Foldio.'

The next Dragon to join in was Theo Paphitis. Christian had always been a fan – Theo was his favourite of the Dragons, both for his style and his business acumen, but if anyone was going to take a hard line on Christian's project, it would be the man who saved Ryman, the national high-street stationery store. Theo began: 'You're probably aware that I might know a little bit about this product. Can you just tell me exactly where you've got to now in the manufacturing and production process of the range?'

Christian replied: 'As it stands here now, I've approached four manufacturers. With the most competitive obviously being in China.'

Theo asked if he had applied for a patent and Christian said he had two patents pending, with six registered designs and a Foldio trademark which covers all the ranges.

Theo was reassured: 'I am totally blown away by the fact that you have developed these products, applied for patents, got prices from the Far East and got to the position you're in. Totally blown away. I think you've done incredibly well.'

Christian was delighted. Behind his concise statements lay a history of dedication and application. It had taken a lot of experiments, trial and error to perfect the idea of the Foldio. How could he halve the size of unwieldy pieces of paper and have them come out of the Foldio perfectly flat? In early prototypes, he had discovered how to fold big sheets of paper around an insert without them creasing. Yet they kept coming out curved. It was only when Christian researched the effect of heat on paper that he was able to adapt the insert to keep everything inside his invention at room temperature. Now, when paper came out of the Foldio it was perfectly flat, but Christian desperately needed protection for his idea.

'There was a lot of work after the development of the folder to do with patents and trademarks and registering designs. The idea of this as a business didn't really cross my mind at first because it wasn't really something where I considered whether it had been done before. It wasn't until I did that research that I realised there was potential for this product to be patented. If I could get everything covered, I could fill a niche in the market and have a real business in my grasp.'

Christian had made some money from his import business, but his funds were limited. To cut lawyers' fees, he looked on-line and filed all the initial patents and designs himself. With equal flair, he formed a brand and a product line, printed off his own brochures, letter headings and business cards and started approaching retailers as a salesman for the company. Meanwhile, he was looking for the right manufacturer – in China.

'It was all through days and days of research, spending 24 hours a day on the computer, just trying to find the best people that could manufacture it, negotiating left, right and centre to get the right supplier. Then Staples and WH Smith wanted to place quite a big order and it all got serious.'

With retailers biting, Christian put the last of his dwindling funds into official patents drawn up professionally by lawyers. Theo Paphitis was impressed. It seemed that Christian's pitch was going perfectly. But then – disaster. Acknowledging Theo's success at Ryman, Duncan Bannatyne, Deborah Meaden and Richard Fairleigh all declared themselves out. Richard voiced their sentiments: 'We've got the supreme investor here who knows a hell of a lot about it. So I think I'll leave it to him and wish you luck.'

Only Theo and Peter were left and though Christian kept his cool, there was more at stake than even the Dragons imagined.

Now, with three Dragons gone, and no bank willing to finance a teenager, Theo and Peter were probably the only two people in Britain who might take a chance on Christian.

Theo said: 'You value your inventions and your designs quite heavily ... I think some of your figures are very optimistic. I think the product's OK, but I'm certainly not interested in giving you

£80,000 for a 15 per cent share in those products. So talk to me about the percentage you're going to offer me.'

It was an agonising decision for Christian. So much work and now he must give away more than he'd bargained for. He had to draw Theo in though. He didn't want to underestimate his intelligence or his knowledge and decided to come straight out with what he was prepared to offer. He said, 'Thirty-five per cent.'

Theo pressed him: 'Thirty-five per cent of what?' 'If you were to back me then I would offer all of my inventions and all of the investment ideas that I have under one company,' said Christian. Theo replied: 'Then I would be prepared to give you the £80,000.'

Christian breathed an incredible sigh of relief. Theo was his idol and role model and it looked like they were going to be in business. Then Peter Jones made a dramatic intervention:

'Hang on a minute. Christian, you're giving away a lot there. I would like to put up half of the money and give you back 5 per cent.'

Peter Jones and Theo Paphitis had invested together in the past. Perhaps this would be a dream combination for Christian. He would keep more of his company and gain two seasoned investors. But Theo was not happy.

'When I invest in people, it's for me to show my generosity depending on their performance. I don't like that to be dictated by anybody else. I'm quite happy to stay with my original offer to you. I'll give you the £80,000, I'll support you, I'll mentor you. I'll put this product out quicker than anyone else and develop your product range.'

Christian hesitated, but only for a moment. That day, he walked out of the Dragons' Den minus 35 per cent of his business but with the huge bonus of an £80,000 investment and the most highly experienced investor in his field. He was delighted: 'I'm quite innovative and I like to create new concepts and new business ideas. Theo's got so much business knowledge. The two put together – there's so much potential there!'

Theo was equally impressed. 'Have you ever seen a 19-year-old stand up in front of you like that? I tell you, I employ people and pay them a fortune to get to those kind of stages, and this guy just turns up at that age and he has done all that.'

Since that day, a lot has changed for Christian. Not all of it has been easy and the learning curve has been steep. At times, he felt that the development process had gone back to scratch and the sheer contrast of new working methods in a big company might defeat him.

'It's so different because I'm used to doing it all by myself. There can be a lot of conflict if there's a lot of people involved. It's a culture shock and I think people have got an issue with my age as well. If I say to someone, we need to get this or that done they can take it personally because they have been in business for much longer than I have.'

Fortunately, at the crucial moment, Theo stepped in to point Christian and his team in the right direction. 'There was a lack of communication and finally we had a board meeting where I spoke to Theo. He flew me over to China and we got it all sorted out over there.'

Now that these initial hurdles have been surmounted, Foldio is on course for launch. Christian acknowledges the extra phase of development has resulted in a whole range of products of different sizes aimed at a variety of users.

'We've got one range that appeals to students and another that appeals to the professional market. We've got a lot of architect firms interested – one of the biggest in the world is ready to place an order for all of their employees. The A1 folder is probably my favourite because the paper folds twice within it so you're reducing it by about 75 per cent. That's going to be one of our best sellers because if you've seen people walking around with those big A1 folders you'll know they really struggle!'

Until the product's launch in the summer of 2007, Christian will make no money. To keep him going, Theo has put him on a minimum wage. Christian is fine with this – it is more than he would have been getting if he had not risked the Dragons' Den – and his pleasure in Theo's support is evident:

'Theo is straightforward. His target is to sell as many of the product as possible. He always speaks his mind which I really like about the meetings we have – it really propels the whole process of getting things done. He's got the reputation of ripping products apart and finding out what's wrong with them and the vision to see two or three steps ahead, not only for the product but for the whole business.

'I'm in the process of patenting quite a few other products in a completely different realm now and Theo's advice is invaluable.

He's really invested in me. He always made it clear he wanted to mentor me, not just develop one product and one company.

'The best form of learning something is through actually experiencing it yourself, having the kind of stress you get with trying to launch a product. It helps to learn the processes rather than study a text book, the internet or a diploma in business. Theo helped me find a realistic approach and changed my view on everything.'

Theo Paphitis has invested £80,000 and a great deal of time in his young entrepreneur. He has a characteristically wry and down-to-earth view of his protégé's journey so far. 'Christian has still got a long way to go. He appeared on a television show, some bloke in a dark suit with glasses agreed to throw some money into his project. But that does not make it a success and it does not make him an entrepreneur. All that has happened is he has just got somebody to agree to invest in his dream. What is important for him to realise is that I do not want to run his business, he has to make it happen. That is a true sign of an entrepreneur – not just turning up on TV.

'My hope now is that he is going to finish it off and we are going to have it in the stores. Chris has the drive and ambition to get the product manufactured and make it available. He is very lucky he has got a tame shopkeeper but he is the one that will push this through. What he needs to do is worry about everything. That's the key – worry constantly and assume nothing! Think about margins and product delivery and brand. Then once it is ready, he has to market the project as hard as anyone can. It is going to be a great lesson for him!'

DUNCAN BANNATYNE

Duncan Bannatyne is the energetic Dragon who always jumps up to try the products in 'the Den'. His fellow Dragons may tease him about his Glaswegian accent, but they certainly appreciate his clever investment strategy. Duncan has a sharp eye for the best people. It is the individuals that attract his interest when he is looking to invest.

My involvement in *Dragons' Den* has always been an immensely enjoyable experience. First and foremost it has been enormous fun to assess such a wide range of fascinating pitches, from the sublime to the ridiculous and everything in between. I have also learned a large amount both from my fellow Dragons and the pitchers themselves. Previously, I had started companies myself and built them up but I also invested and turned around failing companies such as New Life Care Services Ltd and Alpha Radio, so to be handed the opportunity to study new projects from a different perspective has been a valuable exercise.

As Dragons, it is fair to say that the five of us have many common traits; after all, we are all successful entrepreneurs so there are bound to be similarities. There are differing levels of expertise within the group and I've certainly learned from the insights of the other Dragons. For example, if I ever want advice on retail I will ask Theo Paphitis. He once taught me something about retail that I have not forgotten. He explained a product that can be hung on a wall in a shop takes up no space at all, so even if it only makes a few hundred pounds per year it's been worth it. However, if you want to sell something large, like a lawnmower, you have to make sure that it makes a decent profit because it is taking up a lot of valuable floor space. It's simple logic, really, but such an important aspect of retail.

Deborah Meaden is an excellent marketer. She really under-stands the concept of letting the public see what you do and I was particularly impressed with the way she dealt with Steve Bellis' proposal to take his in-pub Poker League nationwide because she instantly recognised how breweries love to have events in their pubs so that they can sell more beer.

In my opinion, Richard Farleigh was by far the cleverest of all the Dragons. His analytical mind is demonstrated by the fact that he is a chess champion and I think he has a precious ability to proj-ect into the future. He's probably invested in more struggling companies than anyone I've ever met and he's very good at it. He can turn businesses round, befriend people, work with them and turn an investment into an enjoyable experience. I've made two investments with Richard and he's a pleasure to work with.

Peter Jones is very knowledgeable and he's built up a good business of his own. He possesses a real variety of skills but perhaps most importantly I think he has the most drive and ambition of all the Dragons. We all have a certain motivation – we had to get where we are now   but I believe it is a quality that tails off with time, especially once a person reaches their 50s. It certainly did with me. When I was Peter's age I had a Rolls-Royce and was driven round by a chauffeur and all that kind of thing. I was ambitious and was constantly starting new businesses even though I started relatively late, at the age of 30. These days I love my life, my wife and my children and I enjoy fantastic holidays, but that drive is still there. Like all entrepreneurs I have a low boredom threshold and I always have to be doing something. I cannot sit at home just watching television – sometimes I wish I could! We all have that particular zeal and a total belief in ourselves. I believe everybody can do what we have done, but they won't. Why don't they? I don't know.

It is difficult to know how and why the Dragons became involved in business in the first place. In my case, I had no choice. I had no job, so I created one for myself. It was either be a road-sweeper or start my own business, so I did the latter. We come from different backgrounds and because we all have our own businesses and our own ideas about what works within business, we all have particularly strong opinions borne of years of graft and decent results.

Some have suggested that entrepreneurs are often people that have problems with authority and that is why they are so determined to become their own boss. I'm not really in agreement with that. As Dragons we can be short and sharp sometimes, but I think we have problems with incompetence rather than authority. If we have invested in a company then we want to be able to have our say. When I can see where a company is going wrong I want to get in there and fix it.

Dragons' Den is entertainment, of course, but at the same time it is still business and I'm always sitting there just listening and hoping that I'll see an opportunity. Too often there's no opportunity and I have to tell the pitcher, but I am always hopeful. I certainly have an inclination towards the service business because that is where my expertise and experience lie, but when it comes to the pitcher I search for genuine enthusiasm and honesty. Occasionally someone will present a product that I love, that I'd like to buy, but I believe that it will not make any money so I decide not to invest. For example, one group pitched a hat that covered your entire head and would help ease the pain of migraines. I wanted one because I do get migraine headaches, but I could not see it being a big seller.

There have been some truly awful products in the Den that turned out to be great entertainment. For a long time I thought the idea for cardboard beach furniture was the stupidest product I ever witnessed. It was a concept that fell down immediately when I pointed out what would happen if you were wet from the sea when you sat on it, but even that was superseded by the right-hand glove man. His idea was to market a glove that you would wear on your right hand when you go to the Continent to remind you to drive on the left-hand side of the road. I suggested that he market another glove so that when you come home from Europe you can wear it on your left hand to remind you to drive on the left. He admitted that was a possibility, so I replied: 'Well then, you've invented a pair of gloves. Fantastic.'

I have never regretted not investing in an idea from the show, although sometimes we have been accused of being too dismissive too quickly. There was one company called Cabtivate that wanted to put televisions that would screen adverts in black cabs. All of us told him he was crazy, but soon after the programme aired he started claiming he had proved us wrong by signing a £5 million contract. He was trying to convince the world that he had put one over us, but we were proved correct in the end.

There are certain types of businesses that I will refuse to invest in. For example, I once received an e-mail from someone with an idea that would make it easier for pubs once the smoking ban was enforced by providing a new kind of area for people to smoke in, but I think smoking should be banned in the streets, it should be banned in gardens, it should be banned everywhere. We shouldn't allow it outside a person's own bedroom. So naturally I refused. On other occasions I will not invest simply because I believe it will be too much hassle. I was given the opportunity to get involved in a property in Romania, but I know all about Romania because I have a hospice there and I know what hard work it is in that country. There would not be much chance for profit or fun when investing in Romania – I would rather just give the money to the country than try and make a profit from it.

One of the inevitable consequences of working on *Dragons' Den* is that every single day I receive countless e-mails, letters and other correspondence from people asking me to consider investing in their ideas. I have never chosen to become involved with any of these projects. Some are crazy, some are ludicrous, some just unbelievable. One person claimed that he had managed to harness the power of gravity and turn it into a mechanical force. This is a classic example of an idea I am not going to proceed with purely because I do not believe that the person can back up their claim.

Over the years I've received some real classics. One group wanted to market a sort of paper pocket to restaurants and cafes that held individual knives and forks. Someone else wrote to me claiming that he had developed a method of winning competitions that was 99.9 per cent successful. I could not understand why, if it was so profitable and reliable, he was in need of investment. There were no details of his revolutionary system included. One idea from America was for a series of connecting bars that you place into the boot of a car to help with storage. I could not deny that it might be helpful in stopping items from rolling around too much in the boot, but it was hardly revolutionary. I particularly liked one section that was headed: 'Target Markets.' Underneath it said: 'Owners and operators of vehicles.' Brilliant.

There have been numerous other proposals as well, from the offer to market an old family salad-dressing recipe to the notion of selling wine in a can. I've been asked to be involved in spas, fisheries and a biofuels business. I even received a complicated proposal regarding Caesarean births! One lad wrote to me asking for financial help in establishing him as a London tour guide. I am sure there are successful tour guides out there and there are some fascinating historical walks to be taken in London, but this gentleman proposed charging £200 per person per day for the privilege of his company. 'What marks me out,' he explained helpfully, 'is that I know the London Underground like the back of my hand.' Presumably he was not aware that tube maps are available to everyone for £200 less than the price of his tour. Another scheme was concerned with the legitimate problem that many young people have little chance of raising the deposit to buy a house. They wanted to start a scheme where they would sell raffle tickets priced at £100 to give young people a 1 in 8000 chance of winning a house. There were so many flaws in this idea that I barely knew where to start. So I didn't. I read these sorts of things every day.

So, if those were the bad examples, what helps make a really strong, profitable business model? What would impress me on *Dragons' Den*? Here are some of the most important elements.

DUNCAN'S DRAGONS' RULES FOR SUCCESS

• **LOOK AFTER THE PEOPLE** I always believe people are the most important aspect to a business, so I look for drive, enthusiasm, knowledge and someone who I believe I can work with. Personally, I am good at giving people enough rein to manage a business and do the job. I can recognise good managers from bad, but if a manager needs to be straightened out, I leave that to other people. I'm not one for dealing with the public, either! Leadership is part of this section too. People must believe in you and believe in your direction and strategy. This was vital to our success with both the health-club and the nursing-home businesses, where everybody pulled together because they truly believed in what we were aiming to achieve.

• **CARE ABOUT YOUR PRODUCT** The actual product or service is of course vital. There must be a demand or a need for whatever you are selling. For example, with Denise Hutton's Razzamataz business I knew there was a market for the schools because Stagecoach had already successfully proved the point in this country.

• **IDENTIFY YOUR ORGANISATIONAL STRUCTURE** This has to be right for the business to be profitable. It is possible to go into a company and crack organisational problems but it can take time. Actually, I relish going into a business, identifying the problems and then solving them. A business with problems that I'm investing in is not altogether a bad thing for me because once I solve the problems the company will be worth more.

● **LOOK AFTER YOUR SUPPLIERS** Every business must have reliable suppliers that look after you and your customers. It's simple – the customers are the most important part of the business so make sure you are in the perfect position to keep them happy.

● **COMMUNICATE** We use e-mail in a round-robin system at my company, which gives everyone the opportunity to study changes in strategy or read about general improvements. Communication is a key element because as soon as you start running a business the business gets bigger. If you do not have the correct procedures and communication lines in place, then it will all fall to pieces. This rolls into technology and even though I am something of a technophobe I recognise the importance of effective, modern technology, so I employ people to sort that out for me. Sometimes it's very good to know your own weaknesses!

A LESSON IN FRANCHISING:
DENISE HUTTON'S RAZZAMATAZ

In January 2006 Denise Hutton appeared on Dragons' Den *accompanied by an enthusiastic troupe of child performers in an effort to secure an investment in Razzamataz, her small chain of theatre schools. The company was already well established and turning a yearly profit at the time of the pitch, but Denise was ambitious and eager to expand further. Her story reveals how the drive and enthusiasm of just one person can create a thriving business.*

The entertainment industry has been part of Denise's life for years as she trained in and studied numerous forms of dance, as well as gymnastics, from a tender age: 'I entered lots of competitions, but basically it was my life, all weekend and pretty much every night of the week,' she recalls. As her career progressed she became a professional dancer, performing in cabaret on cruise ships, holiday camps and so forth, and also became a choreographer. Unfortunately, it is a harsh reality that a dancer's working life is cruelly short. Denise admits: 'When you reach 27 you find yourself working with 19-year-olds and although I was still very fit it made sense to plan ahead.'

There were other salient considerations too, and after Denise sustained a couple of injuries it was brought home to her that a self-employed dancer does not earn much of a living when inactive. 'I had always done well at school but I didn't go to university.

I thought about running my own business but didn't really know what direction to take,' she remembers. It was while working in Cumbria that she took her first steps towards building her empire.

It began chiefly as a hobby, a theatre school teaching dance, drama and singing to children of varying ages for three hours on a Sunday before attending her usual job. Very quickly, however, it became obvious that there was a phenomenal demand for the service, that it was a profitable business and, most importantly, Denise found real satisfaction and enjoyment from teaching kids and giving something back to her local community. She soon established a second school on Saturdays in Carlisle and achieved immediate success: 'As soon as we were open it was full,' she remembers.

Using flyers and posters while simultaneously sending press releases to local newspapers, Denise's marketing for the service was simple yet effective and it was evident that there was a market ready and waiting for Denise's school. This compares to the early phases of many of Duncan Bannatyne's businesses – Denise recognised a call for a particular service in a particular area and she capitalised on it. She now had groups of children ranging from 5 to 17 years and while Denise took care of the dancing she also employed specialist singing and drama teachers as well as a fourth member of staff to help out where needed. Cleverly, Denise used her contacts in the professional entertainment industry to hire quality teachers who shared her enthusiasm and who she knew she could trust to make the business a success.

The triumph of these first schools resulted in Razzamataz

expanding fairly rapidly. Denise opened two more schools and as she was about to open a third she realised that the business was growing faster than she could manage. Fearing that potential competitors would recognise her growth and prosperity and jump aboard the gravy train, Denise knew that the only way to move forward was to franchise, a process that she instigated in 2006.

By the time she appeared on *Dragons' Den* in February 2007 she had already sold franchises in Glasgow, Edinburgh and Cumbria, with another one about to open in Derby. Denise remembers her feelings at the time: 'I was terrified but excited. I'm always up for a challenge though – you have to be when you run your own business – and I knew this was a major opportunity for us. I was slightly anxious over whether appearing on the show might damage my business somehow, but I was confident because we had been running for seven years and it was already successfully franchised. I had a lot more going for me than some on the show who appear with just an idea or a company in its infancy.'

The pitch itself was a savvy piece of marketing. Perhaps seeking to tug at the heartstrings of the usually stony-faced Dragons, Denise led a troupe of child performers onto the set. It worked too as Richard Farleigh looked delighted at the prospect of a performance, Theo Paphitis and Deborah Meaden could not help but smile benevolently and even Peter Jones appeared ... well, tolerant, at least. Denise began her pitch by explaining the nature of Razzamataz's business: 'We aim to develop the children's confidence, improve their health and fitness and provide a safe and secure resource for parents.' She asked for £50,000 for a 25 per cent share of the company and then turned the troupe loose to present their catchy Razzamataz marketing jingle, written by an eight-year-old student of the school.

After dispatching the children following a glowing round of applause, Denise reeled off the key facts and figures:

- The franchisees pay Denise a one-off fee for the new territory of between £5,000 and £10,000 plus 10 per cent of their turnover thereafter.
- Her annual turnover was £40,000 with expenses of £10,000, leaving a net profit before tax of £30,000.
- The children come to the school once a week for three hours, paying a maximum of £5 per hour. There are 25 in each class and 75 per school.
- There are 12 weeks in each term and three terms per year.

Denise explained she would use any investment from the Dragons to open 10 more franchises in the UK, then re-invest the money to set up 10 more the following year and then re-invest again to set up 20 more the year after that to establish a chain of 50 schools in total. She claimed it was a good investment because the franchise was already proving successful and projected that the investor would receive their £50,000 back at the end of year three plus a profit of £40,000.

Theo Paphitis was the first Dragon to wade in, clarifying that Denise owned four schools and had franchised a further six. Next came Duncan, who questioned Denise closely while displaying an obvious interest in her business. He revealed that his own children went to Stagecoach, whom Denise diligently knew were the largest competitors in the field with over 600 schools across the UK. Duncan was keen to obtain some precise figures and Denise expounded that her annual pre-tax profit had grown from £18,000 in 2003 to £20,000 in 2004 and £28,000 in 2005. Lastly, Duncan enquired as to whether Denise was taking a salary, the answer being that she had not at first but was now that the business was running viably.

It appeared to be fairly plain sailing for Denise at this point. She had presented an original pitch, was confident in her facts and figures and seemed to have impressed Duncan, but no one has an easy ride in the Den and the other Dragons were intent on turning up the heat. Peter Jones asked how she would utilise any investment and Denise admitted that the cash would help her set up franchises because she could offer the cash to potential franchisees, thereby eliminating the need for them to approach a bank. Instantly, Theo was unimpressed. After confirming that prospective franchisees were not finding the £5,000 fee a stumbling block, he retorted: 'If that's the case then you should totally forget about lending the money yourself because you take away one of the key pivotal points of franchising – the financial commitment they give you from day one.'

Sensing blood, Deborah Meaden moved in for the kill, asking whether Denise had really decided what to spend the £50,000 on. The Dragons were not questioning the viability of Denise's business; rather they were concerned that her vision of the future was not sufficiently clear. Denise almost made a fatal error at this stage as she showed a modicum of weakness, admitting that she had hoped the Dragons might be able to provide some brain power as well as financial backing. Theo was aghast: 'This is not an advice bureau!' he retorted.

'And we're not here to run your business for you', added Deborah before confirming that she was out of the deal mainly down to Denise's lack of clarity and focus. Meanwhile, Peter felt any investment would not be in Denise, but in the people Denise was planning to lend to. Having never met these franchisees, he decided it was not a risk worth taking and he too bowed out.

Richard Farleigh was thoughtful and considered in his appraisal of the pitch, but although he praised the presentation and Denise's business he felt that the mighty presence of Stagecoach as a main competitor was too much. 'As an investor,' he said, 'I don't see the return.' Theo confirmed that he believed Denise needed to consider her strategy carefully and was not convinced that her plan of franchising by lending was correct, noting that it should be the sale of the franchise itself that generated income.

From a promising start, Denise now had to pin her hopes on the last Dragon. Fortunately, Duncan was in a bullish mood and displayed few doubts. He explained that he had invested in Stagecoach in the past and had done very well when he sold his shares. 'I know how Stagecoach works and I think with your enthusiasm you could possibly build the second Stagecoach,' he said. With the caveat that Denise's profit figures had to be correct, he offered to invest in her company at the level she was asking.

Denise was understandably delighted, commenting: 'It was only Duncan that I actually wanted to invest in the company. I'd done a lot of research into him and he's invested in chains and the service industry before. The others were more into gadgets, things you can touch and feel and put on a shelf.'

Duncan was equally pleased with the outcome: 'Peter and Theo spent a lot of time telling Denise that she didn't need any money. Well, isn't that a fantastic time to invest in a company – when it doesn't need the money? I'll put £50,000 in and if it does-n't need the money, the company will expand and we'll just profit from the dividends. Fantastic! How can you go wrong? There was no reason not to invest. In previous years Denise had made a £28,000 profit, so in my mind the business was worth about £200,000 to £300,000. She wanted £50,000 for 25 per cent. It was a no-brainer, which is why for the first time in *Dragons' Den* history I made the investment without negotiating the equity. She was selling the company too cheap and it was crazy that the others did not see it.'

Yet it was not just the apparent opportunity for profit that attracted Duncan to the company. As a Dragon who often values the personality of the pitcher even above the product or service itself, Duncan was impressed by Denise's attitude. 'You could tell Denise was a very honest and decent person. I knew she was going to be great to work with and I was going to enjoy it,' he later remarked. 'Denise didn't have a great business mind but she knew her business and she was so enthusiastic about the service that she wanted to provide. I knew I could help and assist her. Also, I like the opportunity to prove the other Dragons wrong!'

The pair also had something else in common – a real passion for the service that Denise wished to provide. 'I really wanted to get involved,' said Duncan. 'The rise in obesity in children under 12 in this country is alarming. If you get the children into Razzamataz on a Saturday morning where they're dancing, singing, using energy, that is fantastic. How can it ever be anything other than a great company and a great asset to this country and our children?' Denise, too, is quick to point out the advantages her company offers to kids: 'It's confidence-building. Whether the kids want to be singers, dancers or actors, it's just life skills; it improves confidence and helps them communicate with other children and adults.'

The belief that Duncan held in the business has so far proved prescient. In 2007 Denise launched seven more franchises and hopes to open 15 more in 2008 as part of their expansion plans. With Duncan owning more than 60 health clubs in the UK it also made sense to Denise that they should try and combine their resources to some extent. To this end, both hope that some franchises may be opening up within Duncan's health clubs, creating a perfect synergy. 'I know I have a couple of clubs that have got crèches that have closed down, and the crèches are lying empty. So they would lend themselves to what she's doing very easily,' agreed Duncan.

Alongside a marked increase in requests for franchise packs, the positive publicity of gaining investment from a Dragon also led to an unexpected bonus for Denise. In spring 2007 Razzamataz signed a three-year contract with Thomson's Holidays that will see the theatre school operate in Thomson destinations overseas. Duncan was understandably elated, describing the deal as 'phenomenal'. The children will visit the school in the hotel for a couple of hours, three days a week and at the end of the trip put on a performance for the parents. In the summer of 2008 Denise expects to send ten teachers to these resorts as part of the agreement.

Despite the fact that it is still early days for Duncan's investment it is clear that the expansion plans are flowing smoothly. Denise currently employs 15 part-time staff plus an assistant but admits that within a few months she will be able to afford some more help at her head office. 'At first you do it for the love of it,' she says, 'but I've also seen an opportunity and I'd be lying if I said I wasn't in it for the money and would like to be successful.'

No one can deny that she is achieving that success, but as an entrepreneur herself, does Denise have any advice about forming a thriving franchise?

'I believe if you do anything in life then do it properly,' she begins, before advocating employing a franchise lawyer and a franchise consultant. Refusing to be ruffled by potential competition, she adds: 'We provide a really good service, we maintain our standards and we make sure our whole network has great marketing and great publicity, ensuring we advertise locally and in publications that are sent to schools.' Denise believes she has an advantage with staff as well: 'People in this industry are very enthusiastic and they're very, very passionate about what they do. To see kids develop and give back to you is just amazing.' It sounds simple, but it was Denise's determination, belief and passion in her service that persuaded Duncan to invest in Razzamataz, a company that is rapidly going from strength to strength.

A LESSON IN NEVER GIVING UP:
PETER ASHLEY'S EASY X CHAIR

In August 2006 inventor Peter Ashley appeared on Dragons' Den *with his brand new concept in home fitness, the Easy X Chair. Because Duncan Bannatyne had a personal interest in fitness techniques thanks to his chain of health clubs, this could have been an invention that he might have had some real interest in. Despite a hugely entertaining and memorable pitch, though, Peter did not manage to secure any investment for his fascinating machine, but lack of investment has not stopped more ideas flowing from an irrepressible inventor.*

Peter arrived on the set of *Dragons' Den* from an extremely varied background. An Englishman living in the Canary Islands, he is a qualified civil engineer, a hypnotist and a certified psychotherapist. His real obsession, however, is inventing, a passion he sustains in the Canaries by performing live hypnosis shows on stage both in English and, if needed, with a Spanish interpreter. That his inventions alone do not support his lifestyle at this time does not mean he has not experienced a brush or two with fame and success. In fact, Peter has genuine claims to have been on the receiving end of some bad fortune in the past when it has come to capitalising on some of his ingenious ideas.

'If you go into any fast food restaurant you can get a plastic sachet of tomato ketchup,' recounts Peter. 'Well, I invented that little slit at the top. Going back many years, Silvercream used to have these sachets. You had to cut them open with scissors and I sent them this idea to insert that slit. They thought it was a good idea but it wasn't workable because of the machinery involved. Then about three or four years later it came out and of course everybody uses it now.' That was not Peter's only near miss, either: 'When the British currency changed I invented a couple of discs that could convert pounds, shillings and pence into just pounds and pence, but I stupidly gave it away to somebody and it came out as a smaller version than mine,' he remembers, ruefully.

Peter's decision to invent an exercise chair for the home arose when he was trying to purchase a fitness machine for his home in the Canary Islands. 'The one I wanted was quite nice but it was too expensive and there was something wrong with it,' he recalls. When the retailer refused to budge on the price Peter defiantly elected to design and produce his own machine. Coincidentally, this has echoes of Duncan's decision to establish a chain of health clubs – he had to strengthen his leg after a skiing accident and on discovering that his nearest gym was some distance away he recognised the need for the service and built his own complex closer to home.

As he began his preliminary designs, Peter noticed that many of the exercise machines he had been browsing were too large because most of the area that they cover is not used. He began initially by constructing a type of chair with weights on the back, and despite the fact that this first effort did not work his enthusiasm was undimmed: 'I have been making different shapes, sizes and configurations for several years now,' he admits, 'but eventually I came up with this idea of inventing an ordinary armchair that can do everything a large seven-foot exercise machine can do – leg exercises, bicep curls, bench presses, there's even a bike on it.'

After discovering that it was easier and cheaper to buy steel and important parts for his machines in the Canary Islands, Peter based his production in a small workshop there and has now developed over 70 prototypes. 'I was convinced I had perfected a model,' he says. 'A friend came over and tried it out and was impressed but claimed it looked like a torture chair. I was most hurt, but when I looked at it I had to agree. So I have been making it simpler and cheaper and making it more commercial ever since because having a patent is one thing but making it commercial is something else.' Peter managed to take some steps towards attempting to sell his product on-line, where it was billed as: 'The ultimate in home gym machines. You can work out while watching television or listening to your favourite music. The Easy X Chair really is the lazy way to keeping fit!'

All of which conjures an image of the classic British inventor, beavering away in his garage or at the end of the garden in his shed, with grandchildren ogling him, fascinated, from the relative safety of the house. The occasional muffled explosion or an excited cry of 'Eureka!' only heightens the mystery of what he is up to before he stumbles out, proudly presenting the device that will change the world. It is a romantic notion, but, as Peter will testify, many of the world's most important inventions have emanated from the work of such skilled amateurs.

After years of hard graft, Peter was understandably delighted when he was invited to pitch his product on *Dragons' Den*. 'I had always wanted to market this chair,' he says. 'So many people have broken up their old exercise machines and thrown them away or left them gathering dust in the garage or a spare bedroom. They cannot fit it in their living room and in the end it doesn't get used at all.' Peter felt his exercise chair was the answer to this problem and that he had identified a bona fide gap in the market. Yet despite this confidence he was under no illusions and recognised that it would not matter how good his invention appeared to be, he would have to have some facts and figures to back it up. Diligently, Peter had researched prices for parts from Taiwan and China and pulley wheels from Italy to narrow down for the cost of his invention. He then invested in something extra. 'Everybody says you must have a business plan!' he proclaims. 'I hired an expert to write one out for me which cost about £300, but the whole thing is based on hypothesis so really and truly it does not make sense to me. It is only based on what you *think* you might sell, so if it doesn't sell that much then the whole thing is up the spout!'

He remembers the sensation of ascending the stairs and then standing before the mighty Dragons: 'I was trembling. I literally lost my breath and stuttered a bit but after the first couple of minutes it was fine. They are great guys and we had a laugh together and I really enjoyed the experience. It was great fun.' The business plan was a gonner though. 'I rehearsed my business plan like a parrot but when I got there they did not ask me much about it. A total waste of time!'

Peter's pitch has gone down in *Dragons' Den* folklore as one of the funniest moments on the show. Duncan, perhaps keen to prove his credentials in the keep-fit market, readily accepted Peter's invitation to test-drive his unusual piece of equipment. Greeting our intrepid Dragon was this fascinating contraption, an old-fashioned royal blue armchair with all manner of accessories and add-ons, such as pedals at the front and a bench press system at the back. In truth, Peter had not helped his cause by introducing his product with the help of some photos of another of his inventions, an office chair version which looked almost unfeasibly swish and modern compared to the blue armchair. Gamely, Duncan placed himself at Peter's mercy.

Looking a mite pale and with a grin on his face, Duncan sat gingerly on the chair and began to pedal, pull, push and stretch. 'Peter was such a nice lad,' recalls Duncan fondly. 'But the funniest thing was when I said to him: "What am I working now?" And he said: "Your pectorals." So I asked him what I had been working before and he said: "Um, um, your other pectorals." He didn't know, he just said it!' Meanwhile, the other Dragons were evidently enjoying the spectacle of Duncan bumbling about on this odd device. Duncan tried out another part of the gadget: 'I got on what

I thought was a treadmill but I nearly fell off and he said that it was for walking on, not running on. It was so bizarre.'

Peter, not having anticipated the possibility of Duncan flying off the end of his treadmill, swiftly attempted to ensure our valiant Dragon did not injure himself. Duncan, meanwhile, was about to collapse in giggles in front of the cameras. Finally, Peter Jones could contain his amusement no longer: 'You look like a couple of old codgers in their living room trying to keep fit,' he called. 'The old gits!' cried Theo Paphitis as poor Duncan gave Peter a hug and began to wipe tears from his eyes.

Unfortunately, though, and despite Peter's amusing pitch, none of the Dragons offered to invest in the idea. 'They did not think it was marketable and they felt it needed a little more done to it,' recalls Peter, before adding a little cheekily: 'I thought Duncan might be interested but of course it would a competitor for him so he probably would not want to invest in it!'

Bannatyne's Health Clubs renew all their gym apparatus every four years to ensure they are at the forefront of innovations in exercise equipment. Evidently, Duncan has a keen knowledge of the kind of machines that are on the market and what has proved popular with the customers at his clubs. 'Peter's was not a crazy idea,' he insists. 'There are pieces of kit that have all you need to do to keep fit in the home and are of a decent size, but you don't try and make them into a chair that you put in front of the television. And you had to keep getting out of the chair to adjust the different functions. It wasn't crazy but the equipment wasn't good enough and these days every treadmill, every exercise bicycle, has a television on it anyway.'

'He had no real business plan either,' Duncan continues. 'He thought that somebody would just pick this idea up and run with it. But it was amazing. He carries all this equipment in suitcases and assembles it all from out of a suitcase. He actually contacted me after the show because he wanted to come to my wedding and do a hypnotherapy session with us. I was all for it, but my wife wouldn't let us!'

It is not difficult to understand why Duncan would so keenly invest in Razzamataz but not the Easy X Chair. Denise Hutton could prove there was a market for her service; she had hard evidence that it was already successful and profitable; she was an expert in the field having been involved with dance nearly all her life; she had shown commendable aptitude towards her business; and her notion of franchising was already taking off by the time she appeared on *Dragons' Den*. To Duncan, at least, not only was there little risk that he would not make a profit but he also felt there was significant room for growth. Peter Ashley, however, was presenting an invention that looked somewhat unwieldy and almost alarmingly different from other successful exercise models on the market, a product with no track record, little market research, no real figures to back up his hopes – and when Duncan took it for a test drive he ended up falling off. If Duncan were to invest it could only be in blind hope, or, perhaps, an inspired hunch, rather than actual expectation that Peter would be able to produce a genuinely attractive, marketable machine.

The criticisms of his idea have not deterred Peter. 'The Dragons sit in the Den and you think they are going to slaughter you but deep down I think they are all just human beings,' he says philosophically. After the pitch he returned to the Canary Islands, invigorated and determined, and went back to the drawing board. 'I took everything they said to heart,' he says. 'If they are business people then I have got to follow their examples, follow what they think. So I have redesigned the mechanism four or five times and made a new pressure system that is revolutionary in its own right. It does not need weights and you can put it on the back of an ordinary chair, an office chair or even an invalid chair. So it is a completely new system altogether,' he enthuses.

Pleasingly, Peter has managed to claim a UK patent on his invention, but securing an international patent has not been so easy. 'I spent literally thousands on getting a patent. It is absolutely unbelievable. The British were fine, absolutely incredible, and they helped out throughout the process but the international phase is another thing altogether and is incredibly costly.' The life of an inventor, it seems, is not all fun and games, thinking of ideas and attempting to make them work – there are hellishly complicated streams of red tape to negotiate, too.

But Peter is unlikely to surrender. He says that he has a creative passion and an absolute resolve to succeed in this project: 'It is painful. All inventors are individuals like you would never believe. They all believe in their system and that it is the greatest thing since sliced bread. I took the comments from the Dragons lightly at first, but then I understood their points and now I am progressing because of what they told me. My new pressure system allows you to dial up the resistance you want, you do not need weights, you don't need to leave the chair. I have got loads of other ideas in the pipeline too.'

Despite the disappointment of being rejected by Duncan and his fellow Dragons, Peter remains sanguine about the future. 'If I was not optimistic I would not carry on. It takes over your life, funnily enough!' he laughs.

If there is one thing Duncan does admire, though, it is passion-ate enthusiasm and this is something Peter undoubtedly embodies with his keen belief in the influence of inventors: 'Civilisation has been developed by elderly men in garden sheds inventing things,' he muses. 'If it was not for them we would not have electricity, we would not have television and we would only have half the things we have now because they have all been invented in garden sheds.' Peter Ashley is a classic British inventor. Long may he flourish in that proud tradition and perhaps one day he may even prove the doubting Dragons wrong.

JAMES CAAN

James is already an experienced investor. He brings to the Den the perspective of a born businessman who admits that 'investing money and taking risks is part of my character'. This is his first series of Dragons' Den, so what sort of projects will he invest in, and how will he assess the entrepreneurs?

Whenever I look at potential entrepreneurs, I always say that one of the things they should do is observe the masses and do the opposite. What is unique about your idea? What makes you stand out from the crowd? There are a number of mediocre businesses out there, just trundling along or slowly dying. Take a look at the mistakes they're making and make sure you do the opposite.

What qualities would make me sit up and take notice in the Dragons' Den? Well, for me personal presentation is very important. I remember when I was growing up; somebody said to me that you could always tell how serious a person is by the way they maintain their shoes. That observation has always stuck in my head. A lot of people might say, 'What difference does it make if I wear jeans? At the end of the day you are backing me, not the clothes that I wear.' But in my opinion, the clothes you wear say a lot about you. So, presentation and preparation matter.

It's my firm belief that it is people who make businesses successful, not products or services. If you have the best proposition in the world, it will never take off unless you have passion, conviction and good execution capability. As a potential investor, I try not to get too carried away by the idea, but to keep the balance instead; ultimately it is the individual I am believing in and buying into, as well as the product.

For me, passion is really important. When I look at people I want to know that this person really lives and breathes what they do. Most of our sporting heroes became successful because they lived, breathed and practised their sport, right from an early age-think of Agassi or Sharapova. I think business is very similar. You have got to have that conviction and unquestioning belief in what you are doing in order to be successful.

Another important characteristic is the willingness to make sacrifices. If you are not prepared to put yourself out, and you think success will come to you simply because you've got a great idea, then you are not the person I'm looking for. I need evidence that someone has made, or is prepared to make, sacrifices in order to make their idea successful. Perhaps you don't have the cash – are you prepared to put your house on the line, take out a second mortgage?

Or are you prepared to take less of a salary to demonstrate that you're really committing yourself to the job?

Having watched my own father work far too hard, I'm a believer in the work/life balance, but there are times in business when you have to put everything else to one side and really go for it. You can't be rigid; you might find you simply have to work seven days a week, work late nights, and take work home. It's very rare to find a successful person who hasn't made various sacrifices throughout their journey. You may have to travel, be away from your family. Flexibility is vital if you are to achieve your goals.

What will I be looking for in the ideas that are brought into the Den? The first thing is that I need to know that the idea is tried and tested. I probably won't be interested in something that is just a plan on paper. I need to see evidence that the idea is beyond prototype. I need to know that it has been developed, it works and it has market acceptability. Market acceptability means that it has been demonstrated to a number of people who have come back and said yes, this is something I would like to buy. A would-be entrepreneur has got to show me that their idea has got legs. Then the capital I'm putting up would be to develop the product in terms of manufacturing, marketing, advertising, adding more people.

To take an example of an idea from the Den that wouldn't have convinced me, there was a man with a device that boiled an egg. The 49-year-old computer software expert James Seddon came up with a device called EggXactly, which had more in common with a toasted sandwich-maker than a pan of water. Once placed in the device, the egg is cocooned in a flexible plastic element and heated to just over 100°C and the top of the device glows green while it is cooking and then an alarm sounds when it is ready. James convinced Peter Jones and Richard Farleigh to invest £75,000 for 40 per cent of the equity so that he could develop his product.

I watched the programme and was amazed – the prototype didn't work, so it fell at the first hurdle. Secondly, if he had told the Dragons that he had met with half a dozen retailers – and that they were very interested in the idea, but he needed to demonstrate to them that he could manufacture, then that would have told me that the product was tried and tested and had market acceptability. But without that, it wouldn't have interested me.

I am very much swayed by the individual. To take a highly successful example: a few years ago I was approached by somebody who was the Chief Executive of one of the largest serviced-office companies in the UK. He had ten years' experience, he knew his industry, he knew his trade, he had been very successful in a corporate environment working for large companies. He came to me at a time when the market for serviced offices wasn't doing well. The property market hadn't picked up and the share prices of the established players had fallen. The existing operators were all struggling and occupancy levels were fairly low. I could have given him 50 reasons why I wouldn't have backed him, but some people can make an idea work even against the tide, and I really bought his passion, his determination, his expertise and his experience. From a position of standing still, in three years he built a very successful business where we opened ten centres in central London and sold a company where my partner made millions.

Another example: when I was running Alexander Mann, my recruitment company, a lady called Rosaleen Blair approached Jonathan Wright and myself, where she had originally joined as a consultant. She used to run a nanny agency but she didn't have any real experience in recruitment or outsourcing. She approached me and said that she'd like to develop an outsourcing business. On paper she was a moderately successful consultant who had never developed a large business – but her passions, her drive, her self belief, were remarkable. Against all the odds my CEO and myself backed her because we felt that this was somebody who would make sacrifices and who would also swim the second mile.

She now has big multinational companies as customers, such as Vodafone and Deloitte's, who hand over their entire recruitment human resources function to her. The business she has grown is turning over £300 million a year now and she was recently nominated Businesswoman of the Year, an honour that in the past has gone to Anita Roddick and Marjorie Scardino to name just two. This just proves time and time again that its people who make the difference.

In the Dragons' Den, you have very little time to get to know somebody. The first time you ever see them is when they come up those stairs. You need to make a decision quickly. What you can do is try and identify certain characteristics in that person. Good communication skills are critical – you cannot reach potential customers if you do not have the power to communicate.

Another question I would ask myself is does this person have leadership skills? Building a business is something that you don't do that often. Very rarely do you find successful entrepreneurs who are one-man bands. People who have grown a business have usually attracted quality people to join them. In most cases, when somebody joins your organisation they join because of you, because they have bought into you. A lot of people want to know that they are being led by somebody who is a success or is going to be a success. If you can't demonstrate some degree of leadership and vision then you will struggle to attract the right people to make your idea successful.

Though first impressions matter, you need more than a gut feeling or an instant reaction. When you are investing in somebody it is not a one- or two-week relationship, it's a three- to five-year relationship. You need to understand about their background, about their family circumstances, about what drives them. Of course, the idea itself has to be compelling, but for me the execution skills of the individual are the most important thing.

Like every entrepreneur, I take risks, and not every investment has worked. We recently invested in a sandwich-shop chain, for instance. It was quite a big business and we bought it when it was failing. We made the decision to purchase the business very quickly. On paper, it looked quite compelling – it employed 600 people and had over 60 shops around the country – but once I got into it I realised that actually the product was fairly mediocre and there wasn't enough of a differential in the market. The competition was fierce – on every high street there are ten different sandwich shops. The brand itself was a bit tired and its uniqueness lay in its pricing – these sandwiches were cheaper than all the others. If your uniqueness is price alone, that's probably not sufficiently compelling. So, we couldn't turn the business around, but our analysis afterwards was very useful and very important. You learn more from the ones that don't work than from the ones that do. The business at the forefront of my mind is the one that didn't work; the experience of failure is sometimes more valuable than the experience of success.

I would be quite happy to invest in someone who had failed in the past, because the experience would make them a stronger person. When you're running a business, if you haven't experienced a downturn or the impact of a recession then you haven't grown up in business. When such an event happens, your character and your response are absolutely critical; as they say, even turkeys can fly with a strong wind. If you've only ever experienced a buoyant market, it's not the whole tale. When the market is growing year in year out, even average people succeed.

When a recession hits, the first thing that happens is that the demand for your product and service collapses. Your revenue takes a nosedive and you have got to be very conscious that your revenue and your cost base have to be correlated. If you are selling 100 of something a week, you need an infrastructure to support that revenue, but if next week you are only selling 50 of those things you don't need the same cost base. Therefore unless you have the ability to react and respond to a declining market by rationalising your fixed and variable cost base you will be out of business sooner than you think.

As the chief executive you have a moral responsibility to try to ensure the survival of the business. You've got to be tough; letting people go is never easy, but if you didn't cut the cost base you could lose everything.

Obviously, there are some areas of business I'm more interested in than others. For me, technology isn't a favourite, not because I don't believe in it, but because I don't understand it as well as other businesses. Internet-related businesses are really all about marketing – just because you have a web portal up, how does the guy in China know about you? It needs to be marketed and the cost of marketing isn't cheap. The cost of acquiring new customers in the world wide web is just as expensive as for bricks and mortar businesses.

Retailing is another very expensive and very risky business. Capital expenditure in retailing is huge. I looked at a business recently that had 100 sites across the country and needed a revamp. It would have cost me £50,000 per store to relaunch, so potentially I could have spent £5 million just to give the business a face-lift. But assuming I had done that, would it have worked? There's no guarantee that by giving it a fresh look you are going to increase business. So while I find retail interesting, it's also high risk.

I was nervous about going into the Den, but also excited about it. The nerves were simply because I hadn't done it before. I've done interviews on business programmes and news programmes, but that is very different from doing a weekly episode in a series.

A lot of people have said, 'Are you scared that you are going to put all this money in and it won't work?' Funnily enough that is the least of my concerns because that's what I do for a living. Investing money and taking risks is part of my character, it's what I do. I think the difference is that doing it on TV means that I will be far more heavily scrutinised.

My family love the idea of me becoming a Dragon, though they are a little worried about the exposure. Seven years ago I was featured in the Rich List, and that wasn't much fun because people start to look at you in a different way – the money first and you second.

Several of the ideas in the earlier series have interested me. I thought the iTeddy was an interesting concept. Although Imran had yet to obtain a patent, both Peter Jones and Theo Paphitis saw the investment opportunity. With the growth of iPods that whole area is becoming a big market and I would certainly have been interested in investing.

Igloo the refrigerated delivery service owned by Anthony Coates-Smith and Alistair Turner was also very interesting. In the Den there was a bidding war, with all of the Dragons wanting to invest. I would have joined in as well. Here was a tried and tested business, a business with market acceptability, plus two individuals who demonstrated real belief in what they were doing. What they really wanted was the capital to take their business to another level. All this meant that their chances of success are high.

In my field, I spend 80 per cent of my time trying to understand the downside of an investment opportunity because I think that if you can get to grips with the downside the upside generally takes care of itself. After more than 20 years of experience, one thing I can say with confidence is that in any business situation, anything that potentially could go wrong, generally does go wrong!

There have also been cases in the earlier series where a good opportunity would have passed me by. One I would definitely have got wrong is Levi Roots and his Reggae Reggae Sauce. I would not have seen the potential in him when he sang his song in an attempt to impress the Dragons. I take my hat off to Peter, who saw something there that I would have missed completely and that demonstrates that different people latch on to different things. Another entrepreneur I would have missed was Denise Hutton and Razzamataz, the dance group that was backed by Duncan. My view is that it is a very difficult business to scale up. When I look at a business I ask myself, how could this be national, global and scaleable? But if you read the case study you will see that Denise had global plans and is already taking Razzamataz international.

As an investor, I start the business off and get it to a certain point. Obviously I am looking for an exit, but one thing to remember is that when I am exiting, I've got to leave something on the table for the next guy. If you have got a business to a certain size and it has done well then the person buying it has to believe that it can double and triple again. If he can't see that future growth then you have got no exit strategy. Another point is that you can't sell a business at its peak because that demonstrates that there is nothing left for the next guy.

To any potential entrepreneur I would say, don't go with the wave; find something unique. Always remember, it is your attitude not your aptitude that determines your altitude!

JAMES CAAN'S DRAGONS' RULES FOR SUCCESS

● **OBSERVE THE MASSES AND DO THE OPPOSITE** It is much easier to be part of the crowd than not, but an entrepreneur with a passion may need to swim against the tide.

● **PRESENTATION AND PREPARATION MATTER** This has been said before, but if you do not make the best of yourself how can we believe that you will do the best for your business?

● **IT'S THE PEOPLE WHO MAKE A BUSINESS SUCCESSFUL, NOT THE PRODUCTS** How are your leadership skills? Successful entrepreneurs are rarely one-man bands, and exceptional communication skills are vital.

● **YOU CAN – AND MUST – LEARN FROM FAILURE** Entrepreneurs need to be prepared for things not working out as planned, they have to be prepared to make sacrifices for the business, and be prepared for taking risks. Who dares wins!

RICHARD FARLEIGH

Richard's time in Dragons' Den *has in many respects been an extension of the kind of work he has been involved with since he 'retired' from the world of investment banking. He is a financial expert, but interestingly he doesn't prioritise 'the numbers': he believes the key to finding an investor is a good idea.*

One of the first methods I utilised when I began working with, assisting and investing in small businesses was to scour Oxford University for promising, sometimes superb ideas that were failing to come to fruition simply because of a lack of finance. With my own experience and business understanding, I found I could invest in these ideas and help turn them into reality. In this regard, the set-up on *Dragons' Den* is not too dissimilar although there are stark differences too. The atmosphere and set-up of the Den is completely unique – I have never encountered any situation in my career as a business angel that is comparable. To be honest, in some regards the format of the show runs contrary to how I would usually seek to tackle a potential investment.

I find taking part in these programmes a fascinating exercise. When I was an investment banker I was always asked to undertake interviews with employee candidates because of my rigorous knowledge of economics. I was asked to conduct the interviews specifically to give these people a real grilling about their courses and their experience and it was a process comparable to the one frequently endured by the pitchers in the Den where they are subjected to a comprehensive interrogation by five fearsome foes – well, four fearsome foes and me! I believe I differ from the other Dragons in this respect because I have found time and again that the most effective way to get to know an entrepreneur or business person I am considering investing in is to relax them. I have discovered that a calm, informal conversation is absolutely key to receiving the best and most honest answers.

Of course, such a philosophy is completely at odds with the stressful atmosphere inside the Den. Some of the Dragons can be mercilessly unforgiving in their interrogation but in addition there is the pressure that the pitchers exert on themselves. They are keenly aware that this is the only shot they will get in front of this group, they do not have a great deal of time and there will not be many other similar opportunities. All in all, it's a very special, rarefied atmosphere inside the Den and I really have to admire anyone with the courage to go through with it.

There are plenty of other differences between interviewing in the Den and in my daily business as well. For example, whenever I

meet with a business person presenting me with a potential investment, I will come armed with a decent amount of knowledge of
both the person and their product or service. I will have conducted
some research, formed some pre-conceived opinions and I will
possess a notion of the sort of questions I would like to ask them as
well as the type of information I am looking for. In the Den we
literally have no prior knowledge at all about the people presenting
to us. For all we know it could be Jack the Ripper standing before
us asking us to invest in his business. I cannot check any facts at all;
I do not even have a laptop in front of me that would enable me to
Google and verify certain details, and simply because of the nature
of the programme, there is no personal feeling between the
Dragons and the pitcher, either. The distance between us is quite
significant, so there is no opportunity to really gauge a person's
character on a more relaxed, one-to-one basis. Therefore it can be
incredibly difficult sitting up there as a Dragon – you really must
live on your wits and your instincts much of the time.

Away from the Den I talk to the would-be businessperson about
almost anything other than business. I always liken it to being on a
first date, in that within the first five minutes you can often have a
strong idea as to whether this could be a relationship that might
work out or not. I actually find I can learn quite a lot by keeping
the conversation away from business. I do not care what their
particular interest is, whether it is cricket or snooker or ballroom
dancing; what I'm really searching for is someone who can demonstrate some genuine insight and some proper passion about a

subject, because it's that spark of sheer enthusiasm that I am always searching for. It's often possible to discern this kind of commendable fervour during pitches in the Den, but time is so limited and it is not easy to get through to every individual personality.

When a pitcher ascends those stairs and stands before us I am immediately looking for them to define, within that first minute, what is unique about their business or idea. The fundamental key to a successful business is almost ridiculously straightforward: either it must be something completely new or it has to be offering something appreciably better than the existing competition. It really is that simple. There is nothing else, and it really does astound me that sometimes it takes me an incredibly long time to decide which one of those two things a pitcher is seeking to present on the programme, when it should be the first thing they explain. That lack of clarity can be fatal, so quite often my questions are an attempt to understand why the business in front of me is different. I want them to say, 'I have a new product,' or 'I am going to do this better by …'

An excellent example of a *Dragons' Den* company that did this very effectively was Igloo, whom I chose to invest in along with Duncan Bannatyne. Alistair Turner and Anthony Coates-Smith had decided to enter the business of thermo-logistics and specifically temperature-controlled transport. Now this sounds like a fairly boring industry – it's been around for such a long time and, I suppose, it is a strange business to start up because there will be so many established companies in the marketplace. These two guys are not presenting anything new with Igloo: instead they are purely just doing everything so much better than their competition. I was impressed by their pitch and every time I have spoken with them since, because they are so innovative, so passionate – they had that look in their eyes! It did help, of course, that they are economists as well, a fact that offered added comfort to an investor. They possess a whole host of areas where they can lay solid claim to offering a higher-quality service than their opposition. They have superior software, their marketing is more effective, their trucks and their uniforms are clean, eye-catching and attractive and perhaps most importantly they have a real can-do attitude, a proper willingness to help their clients and an open-mindedness when it comes to alter-ing their service to suit the people that ultimately pay their wages.

I often find that my methods and ideas can differ quite dramat-ically from some of the other Dragons. Some set great store by a pitcher's three-year forecast and quite often we have caught people out because their sales minus their costs does not equal their prof-its, but I have to admit that I have absolutely no interest in that information. Over the years I have seen numerous business plans and I have never seen even one that has come close to achieving the estimates in the plans. These business plans often contain spurious accuracy, where they claim they will sell, for example, 30,357 units in year four instead of saying 'around 30,000'. I am incredulous when I read such figures because there is no way that you can be that accurate. Therefore I find talking about such forecasts a complete waste of time – I'd rather talk about the size of the market, what their costs are and attempt to discover how much they have managed to think about the process of getting the product onto the market.

I have noticed that often one inconsistency or a single mistake made by the pitcher is enough for one or two of the Dragons to pull out of a deal. In my opinion, they often do not allow enough leeway for the state of mind the pitchers must be in. I try not to ever put the boot in to the pitchers because the truth is that I feel sorry for them! There are so many difficult factors that they have to face. The room is intimidating and not only are they presenting in front of us, but also in front of a whole host of production staff. Plus they have to climb those stairs so they will be puffed out as well as nervous when they start their presentation. All this adds up to an incredibly daunting experience so I find myself always trying to make allowances for nerves and intimidation.

I am also often surprised to see Dragons drop out of the running because a pitcher is not completely confident about their figures or perhaps makes a mathematical error or two. I sometimes think about what the Dragons would make of Alexander Fleming if he entered the Den to present penicillin. He would be asked: 'What's your year three forecast? How much will it cost to make? Why are your clothes so funny? Have you got a patent?' He might not have known the answer to any of their questions, but he would still be in possession of a critical piece of research. I have had similar sorts of experiences at Oxford University where some crazy professor will show me an incredible idea but he'll freely admit that he is the last person on earth to try and run a business.

In a case like that, where you have full belief in a product, you have to acknowledge the shortcomings presented to you and perhaps bring in someone who can provide the necessary business skills. A lack of information or particular ability does not mean that an idea should necessarily be completely disregarded. In fact, I look for honesty and I value it. It can be quite comforting for me if a person is honest about what they do not know because often it is something we can rectify or help.

Put plainly, I am not always looking for an accountant. For example, when Levi Roots pitched his Reggae Reggae Sauce on the show he made a gross error during his pitch, but I was not worried because the idea was strong and the sauce was good. There was another occasion where we were presented with an idea called The Knowledge whereby if you were lost you could call a real taxi driver and he would be able to tell you where you were and how to get where you want to go, effectively utilising the encyclopaedic knowledge of cabbies. This was not a bad idea. It may be that it is too late because of the presence and success of global positioning systems, but I still felt it was a reasonable concept. On the show we decided to test it. Unfortunately, when they tried to call the taxi driver no one answered and it was immediately dismissed as a dud idea. I just thought this was such bad logic, because there was no proof that the idea did not work. All it showed was that the guy was, in truth, not a very good organiser. It was amusing, but he just struck unlucky on that occasion. I do not try to catch out or trip up the pitchers; instead I am looking to see whether the idea really could work and how.

An example of one product I particularly liked and invested in on the show is the BakJak, which was designed and presented by Rob Kinna. Rob was a mechanical engineer who was fed up with the discomfort of working on cars, when mechanics have to lean in over the engine and support themselves and therefore only ever have one hand free to complete the work. So he invented the BakJak, which is a kind of support that resembles a sort of adjustable stepladder that allows him to work in comfort. I just thought it was an obvious idea that had not been done before and I was keen to invest because my brother in Australia is a mechanic and I could imagine it being very useful for him. I was impressed with Rob's presentation, too. He was matter-of-fact and did not attempt to blind us with jargon or numbers and if he did not know the answer to a question then he admitted it straight away. This was a trait he shared with the boys from Igloo, who knew their stuff inside out but would never attempt to conceal the truth from us or pretend to know something they didn't. I admired Rob's restraint as well: he was happy to take this product slowly and develop it properly and spend a reasonable amount of money on perfecting it and getting it onto the market.

What I really liked about it was that we could find out so much about whether it might be successful and popular by investing just £10,000 – a relatively small amount of money. I have been involved with some businesses that require millions of pounds to be spent before we can discover whether it is a good idea or not. As smart as we think and we hope we are, sometimes the only way to tell whether an idea will work is simply to start selling it and on this occasion we could do that for just £10,000. You can't manufacture a microchip for £10,000! Fortunately on this occasion our feelings about the project have been proved correct and Rob is doing quite well with his unique product.

A question I suppose all Dragons are asked on a regular basis is whether they ever regret not investing in a particular idea. I have to admit I have no regrets. I try to be disciplined about my role in the Den and I look to play the odds successfully. It's an unfortunate fact that nine out of ten small businesses fail, despite all the best emotions, efforts and hopes, and I am looking for that one in ten that turns out to be a roaring success. Of course I have made mistakes in the past, but those are inevitable, although I suppose I do wish I had invested early on in Skype or Google! On *Dragons' Den*, however, we are seeing a company at an embryonic stage and it is very difficult to judge what could happen in the future; so there is no point in me kicking myself if something I decided not to invest in goes on to make lots of money.

RICHARD FARLEIGH'S DRAGONS' RULES FOR SUCCESS

● **HONESTY AND INTEGRITY** If I am going to work with some-one both as an investor and as a kind of consultant or adviser, I always want to make sure that I am dealing with someone who will be straight and truthful about their business. I would much rather an entrepreneur be completely frank about their shortcomings or weaknesses than they try to cover them up in an effort to impress me. And I like to see integrity – that they really believe in their product or service or idea and are willing to work hard and invest in it to see it come to fruition.

● **ENTHUSIASM** Over the years I have become a risk-taker. If I think an idea is worth the risk I am keen to take it, and one of the signs as to whether a particular investment is worth the risk is whether the entrepreneur presenting the idea has that particular confidence, that certain spark that shows me they are desperate for it to succeed. If they are willing to invest their own money, their own time and their own reputation then these are encouraging signals for me to consider when I assess their idea.

● **WHAT IS IT?** I want to know immediately what the idea is and how it is new or how it is better than the competition. This is such a simple, straightforward requirement for me but it is amazing how many people do not pick up on it or, worse, are unable to explain which one of the two categories their idea falls into.

● **THE MARKET** An idea can seem like the best idea in the world, but if the market is not large enough or is too crowded or already heavily dominated by another company then its chances are obviously limited. I would advise all prospective entrepreneurs or *Dragons' Den* pitchers to make sure they understand their market – the size, how it works and your place within it, because this is simply vital to the success of any company.

A LESSON IN CREATING A NICHE BUSINESS:
ANTHONY COATES-SMITH AND ALISTAIR TURNER AND IGLOO THERMO-LOGISTICS

Anthony Coates-Smith and Alistair Turner set up Igloo to provide refrigerated transport services to food and pharmaceutical companies in the UK. Operating in a mature and competitive market, their aim for the company is, in their own words, to make it 'the best provider of the best service at the best quality – the DHL of the refrigerated transport market'. The Igloo case study explores the issues in changing the transport business from a commodity business to a niche service.

When the founders initially started the business, they had just two refrigerated vans and operated out of a tiny office in North London. For the first 18 months they were out driving vans all day and running the office at night. They took calls from customers 24/7, and remember many sleepless nights – including one in the French Alps, digging their vehicle out of several feet of snow with their bare hands in order to make a delivery on time. In their first month of operations, they earned £2,000 in net sales. Two years later, they had 26 employees and a fleet of 15 vehicles, and monthly net sales had grown to more than £100,000. They had built up a profitable company but they needed investment to accelerate their expansion.

They were confident they could differentiate themselves from the competition. Coming from a food-service background working for big companies, they had been using couriers to transport children's frozen-food products around the UK in a hurry, usually to the catering trade or to journalists and food critics who would write about new products that were about to be launched. If, for example, a new yoghurt came onto the market, the producers would need couriers to deliver a case of each flavour to 20 well-known chefs and writers, so that they could taste it and review it. The producers wanted the product refrigerated so that it was ready to be served, in perfect condition in its packaging, delivered in a courteous manner by a professional-looking company. They did not get what they wanted.

Most of the refrigerated transport services available at the time were operated by sole traders – white-van men offering a glorified taxi service. Anthony and Alistair were spending millions of pounds a year of their employers' money, and getting shocking service in return. They experienced innumerable disasters. Things would go missing when drivers wanted to go home and watch TV – they reported to no one but themselves. They would turn up at food sites, where hygiene was paramount, in dilapidated old vans and wearing scruffy T-shirts, jeans and trainers.

A few companies were providing a similar service but only on a regional basis. One of them might offer a good service in South Wales, for example, but charge a small fortune for a delivery to London because it was outside the operator's home territory.

Horror stories about products being manhandled, kicked about and squashed were commonplace.

Anthony and Alistair decided to move into the market and offer what was lacking – a brand people could trust and rely on. Their vision was a consistent service, carried out to the highest standard anywhere from Scotland to Cornwall, without sub-contracting.

Although food transportation was a commodity business, they saw certain characteristics that would enable them to find a niche. The first of these was fragmentation in the marketplace. The fact that the market had no defined brand or market leader who could offer and guarantee consistency presented itself as an opportunity for them to do just that. There were no barriers to entry – no reason why anyone else could not have done it and no reason why anyone else could not do it today and compete with them. Their only hope of real success was to move fast, grow quickly and push the brand out to as many people as they could possibly reach.

Their value proposition was to offer a significantly better service than their competitors without charging higher prices. By sticking to their key operational principles and high-quality standards, they were sure they could stand out very clearly from the competition in the eyes of their customers.

Anthony and Alistair went to the *Dragons' Den* seeking funding for two new sites – one in the North of England, near Manchester or Leeds, and the second in the Southwest or Wales, around Bristol or Cardiff. In their pitch, they claimed these two new sites would immediately deliver three key benefits. First, they would be able to respond to customers a lot more quickly; second, they would have a more comprehensive UK network, and finally, they would be able to compete on price with local delivery services. They estimated that by the end of year five, Igloo would have a turnover in excess of £5,000,000.

They had kick-started the business with a bank loan of £100,000 secured against their own personal equity. After two years, they had repaid £70,000 of that loan in cash but they wanted to release some of the equity that the business had established to drive future growth. They were turning down work on a daily basis because they could not expand quickly enough, and they did not have access to the credit they needed to grow quickly. They were feeling frustrated because they were running a profitable business and needed capital in order to turn it into something big.

Looking for ways of raising money, they were considering refinancing their houses but did not feel comfortable about the personal guarantees that the banks were demanding of them. They were finding the legal process expensive, arduous and long winded, and it was giving their partners sleepless nights. All in all, they did not feel this was the way things should be going, given that they had grown the business from scratch and it was returning a good profit.

The two partners took the decision to apply to appear in the Den when they were working late in the office one night. Watching the show for a break while they ate take-away pizzas, they found themselves laughing at some of the entrepreneurs. Convinced that they could do better, they decided to have a go. They applied on-line – and were astonished to find themselves in front of the Dragons less than two weeks later.

They stayed in a hotel near the location the night before the filming but were too nervous to sleep. The thought of being in front of the Dragons with cameras rolling, and then being watched by millions of viewers, kept them awake all night. They kept worrying that they would fluff their pitch, or that the Dragons would pick up on something they had missed and make them look silly.

When they reached the top of the infamous staircase and entered the Den, the Dragons – true to form – did nothing to put them at their ease. There were no welcoming smiles, just five scowling faces. The duo launched into their pitch regardless, and managed to get through it. With hindsight, they realised the Dragons themselves were doing a difficult job, assessing a proposal on the spot, on the basis of a few questions and answers without any preparation, market information or background checks.

Anthony and Alistair held their nerve and asked the Dragons for £160,000 for just 8 per cent of Igloo, valuing the company at £2,000,000. This valuation was immediately dismissed by Peter Jones as one of the most ridiculous he'd ever heard. The inevitable grilling came next. Under pressure, Anthony and Alistair were obliged to reveal their vital statistics: 'OK, year one, loss of £70,000. Year two, it turned into £18,000 profit. In year three, we're projecting a healthy margin.'

'Can you give us a figure please? It's hard work …'

'Three hundred thousand.'

'So it's £300,000 – and do you have a bank loan?'

The partners were able to answer almost all the Dragons' questions confidently. There were one or two exceptions. Theo Paphitis wanted to know about their competitors' financial performance. Anthony and Alistair knew all about the services their competitors were offering, and their pricing, but they had not regarded the financial performance of the competition as relevant to their own business. (Their experience in the Den convinced them otherwise, and they did some quick research afterwards.)

Gradually, the Dragons warmed towards them, and Duncan Bannatyne opened up the bidding at £80,000 for 20 per cent of Igloo. Anthony and Alistair rejected this initial offer, which valued the company at just £400,000, on the basis that it was even less attractive than bank finance. Richard Farleigh then paired up with Duncan to offer £160,000 for 30 per cent of the equity, raising the valuation to more than £500,000, but this second offer was also rejected. When Deborah Meaden and Theo Paphitis bid £160,000 for 25 per cent, the show was starting to look like an auction. Not to be left out, Peter Jones said he would match either the second offer as sole investor, or the third offer if another Dragon came in with him.

Anthony and Alistair were delighted to have all five Dragons bidding against each other, showing their support for the Igloo concept. Belatedly, they realised how embarrassing it would have been if all their customers and suppliers had been watching the show only to hear the dread words, 'I'm out'. Finally, Richard and Duncan increased their offer to £160,000 for a share of 22.5 per cent, valuing the business at £711,000, and the deal was done.

The partners signed the contract with their new investors the day before the show was broadcast. The day after it went out, they were inundated with calls from venture capitalists and customers interested in either buying their business or working with them. No less than four competitors offered to sell out to them. Their internet orders soared and they were offered more work than ever before.

In the first six months after their appearance on *Dragons' Den*, they increased their fleet of vans from 14 vehicles to 25, with another 12 on order. Their turnover rose from about £500,000 in the year before the programme to an estimated £1.4 million in the next year, and a forecast £3 million the year after that.

The two entrepreneurs are also happy with the advice they receive from Richard and Duncan. While they do not interfere in the day-to-day running of the business, they do step in when their experience in deals and financing is likely to help. For example, Duncan soon renegotiated the credit terms, halving the company's interest payments and opening up a line of credit with a new supplier. Similarly, Richard got involved when a competitor offered to sell his business and put forward valid arguments against buying it. It was better to spend the money on taking the business competitively.

Anthony and Alistair send their friendly Dragons monthly management accounts, and e-mail them on a more personal note if there is anything newsworthy to tell them. They send more detailed feedback about the business every six weeks or so, and arrange a meeting over a drink every two months to talk through recent developments and share ideas. It is a relaxed way of working together, which seems to work well on both sides. In addition to receiving advice for the business, Anthony and Alistair feel they are learning from their investors as individuals, both as managers and as business owners – honing their skills, evaluating things more quickly, getting sharper, knowing what to look for. At the same time, they believe the two Dragons share their ambitions, their excitement about the potential of the business and the way it is developing and growing, and ultimately the return they will get as well.

Igloo opened a site in Leeds within a few months of receiving the investment. While getting it up and running as an operational centre involved a frantic drive of activity, with major contracts in the area including one for the local council, they were already planning a similar new site in Bristol, to open before the end of the year. As soon as those are complete, they intend to move into other key areas, such as Scotland, East Anglia, Devon and Cornwall. They are determined to keep delivering the sales and the growth that they have promised.

Anthony and Alistair think that there are lots of things that they would like to have done differently but the constraints that were placed on them as a small business opening with no track record, no credit history, no trading history, were too problematic. For example they say:

'Selecting suppliers to service all of our phone contracts would have been a really good move for us, it would have made it easier and a lot less hassle, but we couldn't do that because we couldn't get the credit as a non-trading entity prior to the six months that we had been operating. Nobody would offer us that sort of credit and we had to end up moving from one phone supplier to the next in order to get increased credit. As we were growing the fleet we needed more and more mobile phones for drivers and in obtaining those we felt that 14-year-old school kids probably could get more credit than we could as a business for some reason.'

Anthony thinks:

'Probably the biggest decision that we took that affected the business in the greatest possible way was when Alistair and I took a decision to stop going out and physically doing the driving, the unskilled element, of our job. And the moment we stopped doing that we took a step back, took off our Igloo uniform and put on a shirt and trousers and started going out to meet customers face-to-face, and started talking about what we could do for them as a business. Sales from that point had about a four-week lag, and as our meetings became more frequent with different customers, the sales escalated rapidly. And we went from being a static sort of £30,000 a month very quickly to be doing £80,000 a month. I suppose looking back if I would do one thing differently we should have done that quicker. But at the same time, during those 12 months when we were physically out on the road doing the job we learned so much about how the business should be done, at the coal face if you like.

The things we learned and put in place are still evident today and form the basis on which all of our drivers are trained.'

Their key advice is that 'if you are competing to win business you won't win business by sending a brochure and e-mailing a price. You are most likely to win a relationship with a customer by going out to see them and listening to what they have to say and then building your offer around that and sending it back to them. Once you have got a personal relationship and the person has looked into your eyes, when they want to phone you to offer some work, they are not just phoning the company – they are phoning you.'

A LESSON IN SALES AND MARKETING:
LING VALENTINE AND LINGSCARS.COM

Ling Valentine had been running her business Lingscars.com for about five years by the time she appeared before the Dragons in February 2007. With an entertaining and spirited pitch that managed to crack smiles on even the most stony of Dragon faces, Ling displayed charm and enthusiasm as well as a truly unique eye for marketing techniques. Her personality and skills led to both Richard Farleigh and Duncan Bannatyne offering to buy equity in her company, but that was only the start of the drama.

The story of Ling's career is fascinating: 'I was stuck in China as just another one of the 1.2 billion people competing for a thin slice of a small cake, so, having completed my BSc in Applied Chemistry, in 1996 I went to Finland to continue my studies,' she explains. While in Helsinki, Ling met future husband and business partner Jon through an early version of an internet chat room. Eventually, Ling flew to England for a visit and they drove around Europe together to meet other friends they had met through the same websites. 'Of course,' says Ling, 'we fell in love and that was that!'

After a protracted period of wading through red tape, Ling moved to Britain. While Jon ran a contract hire business, she returned to university and obtained an MSc in Environmental Protection. Finally, a move to Newcastle saw the pair decide to set up their own business and Lingscars.com was born. In simple terms, Ling offers individuals or businesses the opportunity to rent brand new cars over an extended period of time – usually between one to three years, with a mileage constraint built into the agreement. Ling scours car dealerships herself and showcases the best deals that she can find on her cluttered, blinking but delightful website that emphasises friendliness and approachability rather than corporate facelessness and difficult jargon.

The service has many advantages. Customers do not need significant finance to be able to use a brand new car for a few years, there is plenty of choice thanks to Ling's own research and there are attractive bonuses such as free road-tax for the duration of the contract. Quite apart from all that, Ling provides a personal and honest touch that many people clearly find refreshing and reassuring – a fact qualified by over 600 letters and emails of recommendation on the site.

It is Ling herself who is the focus of the branding of the company. 'Everyone always told me I have a weird character,' she explains. 'I am quite forceful and if I want something I just get it. So I thought: there are no Chinese birds selling cars in the UK, so why not simply market myself as a unique concept? I like to have fun and that is what is missing from car sales. I am confident enough that my service is quite simply the best in the UK, so I stuck my name and my head on the website!'

Ling has become justly well known for her bizarre and hugely inventive promotional ideas. The most famous, which Ling show-cased in the Den, is her nuclear missile truck. 'It was really down to Tony Blair and George Bush,' she says. 'They were making so much of the "weapons of mass destruction" and I thought – I can do better than that! So I imported an ex-People's Liberation Army nuclear decontamination truck from China. It's lovely. It cost me £3,500 in total, plus VAT. It arrived on a boat from Shanghai.' Together, Ling and Jon built a missile and branded it with Ling's head and the name of the business. 'I parked it in Sedgefield and pointed it west, towards George Bush,' adds Ling triumphantly. 'When I finally had to move it I received hundreds of letters and e-mails from people saying they missed it!' The Angel of the North, it seems, has some competition.

'I live inside my website,' says Ling. 'It is everything to me. I really wanted the most thought-provoking, useful and entertaining car website in the UK. Being from China, freedom of speech is important to me, so I went out of my way to tell the truth to customers without the waffle. The first thing I did was provide accurate car stock information and clear pricing, because so many other websites simply do not provide these most basic facts. To communicate with customers I employed the same device that Jon and I used when I was living in Finland – instant web chat. I made it a rule from day one that customers could talk to me live on the website and this is extremely popular.'

In the past Ling offered a free lunch, distributed Chaiman Mao

Little Red Books in exchange for poetry from customers, and made short videos in which her sister Shan road-tested various cars for the benefit of viewers. Naturally, the series was named *Chop Gear* and it featured Shan in a Chinese People's Liberation Army uniform explaining the features and advantages of different cars – most importantly, how many Chinese takeaways can fit snugly into the boot. 'BMW have never forgiven me for that,' smiles Ling. It is a site voted one of the Top 100 sites in the world by *FHM* magazine.

In 2006, Ling was the winner of the Women in Retail category at the North East Entrepreneur of the Year awards. 'I share this honour with Duncan Bannatyne who won the equivalent male award in the past,' says Ling proudly.

On returning from a trip to China Ling began to prepare her presentation for the Dragons. 'I wanted a small investment as my business does not eat cash but I was also looking for help with a five-year business plan and an exit strategy. So, having read Duncan's book and researched Richard's success in this area, I focused on these two Dragons,' explains Ling. Most importantly, though, she was determined to make a very special impression: 'Having fun was a real aim of mine. It's pointless to bore the socks off the viewers. I really wanted to entertain the Dragons because I knew I would have a much easier time if they were laughing!'

Many entrepreneurs enter the Den dressed for the occasion in suits or other appropriate business wear. Ling, of course, was never likely to let standard protocol obstruct her own individuality and, armed with visual aids depicting her website and her nuclear missile,

Ling faced the Dragons in combat trousers, a bright orange shirt and a Mongolian fur-trimmed body warmer. The panel were therefore immediately aware that this particular presentation was going to be a little different. 'I really thought Peter Jones would moan, but he never mentioned my clothes,' laughs Ling.

Ling began by directing the Dragons towards the photo of her branded missile truck, a useful ploy to engage their interest as quickly as possible. She then began to explain the nature of her business: 'Contract hire is a very cheap way to run a brand new car. In the US more than 20 per cent of cars are purchased this way, while in the UK it is less than 1 per cent. On my website people can choose the car they want and if they have good credit history the car will be delivered to them. Easy. On average I sell £1 million worth of cars per month and I have made over £100,000 in gross profit in each of the last two years.' Ling then asked for £50,000 for a 5 per cent share in the company, adding that the money would be put towards more marketing schemes, and claimed that by 2010 that initial investment would be worth £400,000.

That was pretty much the end of a succinct and confident pitch, but, her eyes once again on effective publicity, Ling utilised an idea from her website: 'You can trust me that I have good marketing skills and I'd like to remind you of your British saying: "There is no such thing as a free lunch,"' at which point she handed out free packets of noodles, all branded with Ling on the back, to each of the Dragons. Some looked delighted while one or two, it has to be said, looked rather bemused by it all.

Peter Jones led the Dragons into launching an investigation into her missile truck. Duncan clearly felt empathy when Ling said that the council had ordered her to move it: 'Yeah, councils can be like that,' he replied ruefully.

Richard obtained some information about the function of the website and discovered that Ling takes commission from the car dealers. 'I've got to say congratulations,' he said. 'The profit is quite low but the turnover is fantastic.' Clearly, Richard was considering an offer. Peter clarified some details on Ling's monthly profit, discerning that in 2006 she was making a monthly gross profit of approximately £10,000.

Theo was a little more stringent, however, and it was at this point that things began to unravel. Ling explained, a little uncertainly: 'My net profit in 2005 is £70,000. I left it in the business and then in 2006 I used £25,000 of that money for the marketing. I can't do any marketing without the money.' But Theo was still unsure as to the exact details.

'On your audited accounts did you actually show £70,000 before tax and then pay corporation tax on that?'

'I think I paid about £5,000 quarterly on tax. The thing is that I don't do the books.' Theo was distinctly unimpressed and at this answer he exploded in indignation.

'You come here asking for money saying you don't do the books, how do you expect me to give you money if you don't know what you're making?'

This small exchange was almost like setting off a roll of

dominos. Ling protested that her business was clearly making money and was still going strong after five years, but Peter was unmoved and was even a mite sarcastic in his response: 'Your lack of business nous is terrifying. You can't even tell me how much you're making over three years. Can you imagine me giving you £50,000 now and asking what you spent the money on? "Oh I dunno, I bought another missile." You haven't got a full understanding and appreciation of your business. That's my problem. I'm out.' Very quickly Theo expressed his admiration for Ling's abilities but admitted that he was not prepared to invest either.

Deborah, frustrated by Ling's ability to present any plausible financial answers, arrived at the same conclusion as her colleagues: 'You have a lot of what it takes to be a successful entrepreneur but I couldn't work with you because you can't give a straight answer,' she explained. 'For me you've absolutely lost credibility. I'm very disappointed.' Deborah, too, withdrew from any possible bidding.

Ling, however, feels their questioning was unfair: 'At the time, Lingscars.com was a partnership. Consequently, I did not have any corporation tax figure or audited accounts. It's quite impossible for a partnership to provide these and it was unfair of Theo to demand them just to make me look like I did not know how much money I was earning.'

Three down and two to go and it appeared that Ling's appealing pitch had perhaps championed style over substance. Richard, not for the first time, was about to buck the trend. 'I think you're a good business person,' he began. 'You've created a good business with great turnover and you have a good reputation. I have an issue with the valuation, but just to get things moving I'd like to offer you half the money, but it's going to be a completely different valuation to what you're talking about. I would like to offer you £25,000 for 20 per cent.' This was well short of the kind of investment to equity ratio that Ling was looking for, but she remained quiet as Duncan weighed in. Clearly charmed, the Scottish millionaire felt that Lingscars.com could grow into a nice business and matched Richard's offer.

Ling had been looking for £50,000 for 5 per cent – here was an offer of £50,000 for a whopping 40 per cent. Ling did not blink as she refused the offer. The effect was immediate. Theo laughed, Peter gasped and Duncan replied, in disbelief: 'You're turning us down?' It was another example of Ling's headstrong belief in herself and the business. Staring Duncan right in the eye she uttered a line that is now immortalised on her website, where she glories in her encounter in the Den:

'Well, Chinese eat Dragons for breakfast! I would say 5 per cent each, 10 per cent in total.'

Richard was once again measured in his response and between himself and Duncan an improved deal for 30 per cent of the company was tendered. To the incredulity of the Dragons, Ling remained completely unmoved. 'Thank you. I refuse it.' Theo, perhaps surprised that Duncan and Richard had even made such an offer, could contain himself no longer:

'Ling – think about it. It's a fantastic offer. It's an unbelievable offer. Take their money.' Deborah concurred and for a moment it looked as if Ling had a real dilemma on her hands, but she didn't. She thanked them again and she refused them again and retreated back down the stairs.

Explaining her decision, Ling says: 'All I could think about was that I could get that cash in 30 seconds from the bank for no equity stake, and that I could not face giving away a third of my business for that. I had a proven business and they had no risk! After the Den I had some regrets, mainly wondering if I had lost out from not working with Duncan and what I had potentially lost from Richard's end-game expertise, but since my episode aired I have been incredibly busy.' Indeed, her appearance sparked immediate interest: 'Web visits on the night of the broadcast were over 5,000 people, and the next day it was over 10,000. I spent the whole night trying to stop my server crashing!'

While her madcap nature may have stunned and perhaps even put off some of the Dragons, it is easy to see why Duncan Bannatyne and Richard Farleigh were interested in Ling's business. Both of these Dragons place plenty of stock in the people that they are working with. Clearly both Richard and Duncan could see that with a little more guidance and advice, Ling could take her business to a new level.

Even without such guidance, though, Ling's business has continued to grow. She has plundered her appearance on the show for more positive publicity; her company is being used as a business project for A-Level students; she has bought an old London

Routemaster bus which she uses as a kind of mobile promotional tool at large events up and down the country and her website has been voted best non-franchised site by *Automotive* magazine. Turnover has more than doubled and Ling is confident she will exceed £200,000 in commission income at the end of 2007. She has turned down at least ten investment offers and has valiantly fended off advances from large competitors who have taken a distinct interest in her business. 'I don't want to bleed overheads on fancy salaries, perks and overheads. I have remained totally focused on the needs of the customer.'

Business has been booming: 'Since the show I have been working from 6 am to 8 pm and I have been offered more and more cars to sell as my customer base has grown. I have increased the number of premium car brands I rent (at discount prices) and have had offers of other business opportunities.' One deal Ling has completed is an agreement that sees her refer customers to a particular car insurance company in exchange for a monthly fee. In keeping with her commitment to keep costs low, Ling uses this cash to help subsidise the deals on her website.

Ling freely admits that her antics have made her unpopular in some circles, but she refuses to be distracted by abusive e-mails and anti-competitive pressure from within the motor industry: 'Overheads in the new car industry are sickeningly high, and I simply remove these costs for my customers. I ignore complaints from manufacturers and dealers and take all my advice from my customers,' she insists. With her business continuing to bloom and her innovative promotional ideas stretching to offering customers free cash (Chinese Yuan sent in the post), perhaps in time Ling may even force Richard into regretting not caving in to her demands.

PART 3
KNOW THE BUSINESS
BY EVAN DAVIS

THE DIFFICULT QUESTIONS AND HOW TO ANSWER THEM

You've seen entrepreneurs get a grilling in the Den. But the questions are often hard for a reason. If you are going to spend tens of thousands of pounds of investors' money and a few years of your life pursuing your business dreams, you had better make sure you have thought everything through. Here, Evan Davis who presents Dragons' Den *and is also BBC Economics Editor, outlines some of the questions you need to be able to answer.*

I've worked on five series of *Dragons' Den*. I've mentally calculated that in that time I have heard a total of nine different Dragons ask over ten thousand questions to hundreds of entrepreneurs.

And you know what? The same questions seem to keep coming up again and again.

Indeed, there are about 30 questions that emerge repeatedly.

This is not because the Dragons lack imagination. It is because there are certain important issues that you can't duck when assessing your prospects. They come up in different forms for different firms, different words from different Dragons and with varying qualities of answer. But the basic questions keep on coming up, and I've highlighted them in this chapter for you, so you can tick them off one at a time.

There is one general issue that underlies them all: value.

If you'd like to enter the Den with your own idea, or even to create your own business without entering the Den, it's *value* that should be foremost in your mind.

Your goal is to show two things. First, that you have something that has value to your customers (because if it doesn't, you won't have any customers in the first place).

And second, you must also prove it has value to you and your investors (because if you can't make money out of it, it's probably better as an idea for government or charity).

And the 30 or so recurring questions that the Dragons keep asking are all soliciting information on value, in one aspect or another:

- **what** you have that has value;
- **how** you intend to exploit the value;
- **whether** *you* are the person best qualified to maximise the value;
- and **how much** value there is for potential investors.

Unless your meeting with the Dragons is mercilessly brief, these points have to be covered in some form.

Indeed, you can think of the typical encounter as consisting of three main phases covering these issues.

There is the initial pitch, where you try to reveal what it is that has value. Then there is an interrogation phase where you are tested on your chosen business model, your strategy and your own abilities. Finally, in successful cases, there is a negotiation phase where, having ascertained there is money to be made, you and the Dragons fight over the rights to it. So these are the all important questions, grouped under four headings.

WHAT YOU'VE GOT AND WHY IT HAS VALUE

What does your product 'add'?
Describe the experience your product is meant to give the customer, and describe what problem of theirs your product solves.

What is the consumer's best alternative to your product?
Your customers get by without your product at the moment – so they must have alternatives to it. What are those alternatives, and how is your product an improvement on them?

Has anyone else tried this idea or something similar to it?

Surely if your idea is that good, someone would have done it already? If they have, you should know about it, and be able to describe why it didn't work or why you have something better.

Does the business have a natural finite life (like a one-off project) or can it live for ever?

The best businesses go on for ever ... but not all of them. When the contract runs out, when the fad is over, or when the patent expires, the business is over. It had better be very profitable in the meantime.

Will the consumer be able to appreciate the value of your idea, or does it, for example, require the buyer to change their own behaviour?

Sometimes you can have a great idea for helping people, but it's going to take so long to sell it to them, or it requires them to make such a big change to their behaviour, that it's never going to take off.

Has your product been rated by any experts, buyers, competitors or partners?

It's worth mentioning if other people have rated your product well. Especially if they are people in the know. Even better, if they have tried to buy you out. If the only other people who've told you it's wonderful are your friends and family, then don't bother. We can take it as read that your mum likes it.

Can anyone copy it? Or do you have some kind of protection such as a patent?

This is the crucial question. However good your product is, can you stop other people selling it in competition with you? If not, it has very little value to you. A patent, a secret recipe, an exclusive contract, even a registered design or a celebrity endorsement. Something that stops your product being a commodity.

What does your company balance sheet look like and what debts do you have?

If you already own some assets – like property, capital equipment or cash in the bank – then you have something of value, but you do need to subtract your debts from that. Many start-ups have no real assets and no real debts to speak of.

Who are the other shareholders and what price did they pay for their shares?

Investors like to know whether they are paying a higher or lower price for their shares than other investors. If the price is higher, you need to have an answer to the question 'Why?' and that answer needs to show there is more reason to think the company is profitable than before.

Do you have a dependency on other companies for your product? Are you, for example, a distributor for someone else? Do you have any obligations to other companies?

This is important: if you are dependent on another company, it may be that you have no value in your business at all. It's all with them. (If the company you are pitching is dependent on another company in which you have an interest, expect to get a pretty rough ride. You certainly won't get an investment.)

Is your business model scalable?

The Dragons like to know that your business can grow, and can be replicated. Opening a successful shop is good, but not as good as opening a shop that can be replicated in every street in the country.

Is there an international market for your product?

International potential is a big advantage – and you should mention it, but it's best not to go on about it until you can say you've conquered the domestic market.

Are there any regulatory hurdles for you to overcome in order to pursue your business?

Regulations can make or break a business and can certainly limit the competition within the marketplace. You should be more than just aware of it. And you always need to have competent answers to questions on issues like safety certification where relevant.

HOW YOU WANT
TO EXPLOIT IT

**What is your main revenue stream, and do you have
any subsidiary ideas for making money?**

Be clear about exactly how you intend to make your money
– it's amazing how many people wait to be asked – and offer
suggestions for subsidiary money-making opportunities. The
true entrepreneur is one who thinks laterally, about how to
make a second business out of the first.

What is your route to market?

Be clear about exactly how you intend to get your product to
your customers, and what the alternatives to that route are.

**Are there obvious business partners who should take
over or be linked to this business?**

Often, there is a route to exploiting your idea through existing companies. Have you tried to sell your idea to them? Or
license it? That can be far easier than you having to manufacture and distribute your product from scratch.

How can investors exit the business when it is established?

Offer one or two suggestions as to who might want to buy the business a few years down the road. If you say that *you'll* want to buy the business from the Dragons, it's worth outlining how you'll find the money.

How much money does the company need now, and will it need in future?

Be ready to talk about the financing of the business not just now, but down the road too. Investors need to know whether they – and you – will find their shareholdings diluted down to almost nothing by the time the business has found its feet.

What is the best form of finance for you to raise?

Do you need equity finance? If you are simply looking for money to pay for an order you have, you might find the bank a better place to go. The Dragons are most useful for riskier investments.

What will you do with any money raised?

You don't need to have this down to the nearest penny, but some rough guide as to what the money will be used for is useful.

Is the money you are likely to raise sufficient to the tasks you need to carry out?

If you are planning a national TV advertising campaign, asking for £30,000 won't do it. You do need to pitch for as small amount as possible, to increase your chance of securing cash, but you must pitch realistically.

WHO ARE YOU, TO MAXIMISE THE VALUE OF YOUR IDEA?

What does your background, experience and track record tell us about your competence to run this business?

There is an enormous difference between someone who has demonstrated the skills necessary to run a business, and those who have not. But if you have some business failure in your background, there is usually something positive you can find to draw from it.

What do you propose to pay yourself?

Dragons don't like investing a lot of their money in a business to pay you a comfortable salary. Try and keep it to a minimum. Any acceptable salary will be far lower than your worth – your return will come in the form of big profits when the business succeeds.

How much time will you give to the business?

Dragons don't usually like the idea of entrepreneurs splitting their time.

What are your motives – to make money or to achieve something else? To stay in the business, or to exit?

Investors usually want to make money, so it's useful for them to see that you are committed to that goal. Your personal fulfilment is important too – but of less concern to investors!

Are you linked to any other company and if so why is this new one not part of that?

If you have another company, why are you not combining the one you are pitching with that one? The real answer is usually that you don't want to risk the viability of the old company with a dodgy new gamble. It's a hard sell to an investor though.

HOW MUCH VALUE IS THERE – THE NUMBERS

How much can this product sell at?
Offer guidance to the price the final customer will pay, and the price you will sell it at to the distributors.

What is the size of market?
How big is the relevant market for your product? Avoid offering details of irrelevant markets. If you are selling food for hamsters, you need to know how many hamsters there are, not how much pet food is sold.

What does your product cost?
And how much cheaper could you make it, if you tried?

Is there any evidence of actual sales?
The best single piece of news you can deliver about your product is evidence that when offered it, real customers somewhere have bought it for real money. On the hand, if sales have been disappointing, you will struggle to get an investor interested.

If you're building a company, you'll see the questions all come back to what you have of value. It's worth digging a little deeper into what the value means and where it comes from. That gets us into some useful concepts that keep recurring: profit, competition and information. Let's take a look at each of them.

VALUE AND PROFIT

Think of a business as a profit-generating machine.

How much would you pay for that machine?

Well, the answer probably is: as much as the profits you expect it to generate over the years ahead. That's the value of the machine.

When the Dragons (or other like-minded investors) listen to a pitch they are usually looking to partake in the creation of a new profit-generating machine, which they can later sell. When they make that sale, they hope to capture a good chunk of all the future profits that the company will make.

If you can successfully make one of these machines, you are clearly on to something.

But there are two types of profit. There's the normal everyday profit that gets you by – that justifies the cost of building the machine but little more.

And then there's *real* profit, the kind that makes you rich. The kind that more than justifies building the machine. Economists call it 'economic rent'.

If you want to understand the difference between humdrum everyday profits and the real wealth-generating kind, think of David Beckham's salary. Let's, for sake of argument, assume he earns £100,000 a week. Now suppose he wasn't a world-class footballer, what might he be? Maybe an ordinary plumber earning perhaps about £500 instead.

So a good way of thinking about Beckham's salary is that the first £500 of what he earns is the everyday wage that compensates him for getting up in the morning and going to work and not being a plumber. And the remaining £99,500 is pure economic rent.

And you can make a similar distinction for companies and their profits.

The first slice of profit – normal profit – is a mere reward for the work a company does and the capital it employs. It's the minimum acceptable profit, that just compensates the investors for not taking their money and putting it into a bank savings account where they might earn a 5 per cent return without much risk or hassle.

If you can't promise investors that kind of return, your business won't even get off the starting line.

But what investors are really looking for is extra profit on top of that. The cash that more than pays the savings account rate on the money invested.

If the Dragons put £100,000 into a business, they don't necessarily expect it to make money in the first couple of years; they don't *need* mega-profits quickly either. However, if they want to sell their share of the business and to make a big return on it, they do need a promise that at some stage the company can earn far more than the 5 per cent rate of interest they would otherwise get on the initial investment.

Unfortunately, that's the difficult bit.

Everybody wants to generate exceptional profit – but we can't all be exceptional. So what's the key to generating attractive returns?

VALUE AND COMPETITION

Usually, companies can really only expect to make everyday profits. Just as most of us employees can only expect to earn everyday wages closer to £500 a week than £100,000. But it all depends on the degree of competition out there.

The general rule is that if there are masses of competitors and you are just one small player of many, you can only expect to earn a normal profit because intense competition inevitably forces prices down to the level that merely compensates you for the basics of doing your job.

If plumbers earned £100,000 a week, a lot of people would become plumbers and fairly quickly the competition between them would drive prices and wages down.

But when world-class footballers earn £100,000 a week, not many of us can match the talent of a Beckham, so there is no competition to push wages down.

So the key to earning the kind of profit investors are looking for is not just having something that customers want to pay for, but having something that stops everyone else being able to imitate you.

You need more than just a good idea. You need an idea that is competition-proof.

The more special your idea is, the less potential competition it can face, the more profit it can generate and the more value it has.

What kinds of things help you stand out above the competition?

You might have an invention that is protected by a patent, or by a secret design others have not yet worked out. You might have a nice design that others can't copy, or a special brand that has a value in the market. You might have an exclusive contract to import and sell a valuable product into the UK market so others can't compete against you, or you might have acquired the lease to a really excellent site to sell your wares.

You might even just have more skill than your average competitor, an ability to produce it faster, better or cheaper.

There are other things you might have too – but you'd better make sure you have something special if you want to get rich.

Otherwise, be content with the life of the majority of us, operating a business in a competitive market where no one earns much above the going-rate for what they do. There's nothing wrong with that incidentally. It's just that it's not the kind of business that attracts adventurous investors.

The message of this section can be encapsulated by a pithy phrase used by some economists: 'There are no $100 bills on the sidewalk.' Or to re-phrase it in English, 'There are no £50 notes on the pavement.'

The argument is that there's no easy money in business, because if it was easy it would already be taken. So if you see something lying on the pavement that looks like a £50 note, you are probably mistaken. If it was a genuine £50 note someone else would have picked it up already.

So when thinking about the value of your business, you always need to be thinking about why you might have been lucky enough to have found a £50 note on the pavement. Why it has not been picked up already?

Now this finding can be very annoying to entrepreneurs, especially those who come into the Dragons' Den with things that seem like a good idea, but which don't have anything special about them.

Take the example of the two nice men who had thought of the concept of a furniture unit specially designed for putting your worn-but-not-dirty clothes in.

We all know the problem of not wanting to wash something that has only been worn for a few hours, but not wanting to hang it back in the wardrobe with the clean things either. We normally leave it on the back of a chair, or the end of the bed. What a good idea to have a piece of furniture that takes these pieces of clothing specifically.

(Actually, not everyone thinks it is a good idea, but suppose it is for the sake of argument!)

Would these two gentlemen be able to make money out of it? Probably not.

If it sold well, not only could anyone copy it, but IKEA could probably copy it *and* do it better ... Even if the two guys' concept was genius, they'd soon be out of business.

It's a bit discouraging for entrepreneurs to be told that even if it works and customers buy it, it's not a good business, but it happens all the time.

Indeed, the people who are faced with this line of questioning on *Dragons' Den* must wonder how anyone ever makes it in business at all. You can't succeed because IKEA can do what you're doing better than you. But how did IKEA get into that position? When Ingvar Kamprad founded it in 1943, couldn't his investors have told him the same?

Why, indeed, would Henry Ford ever have bothered to start a car-manufacturing operation? Why didn't investors tell him that once he succeeds, other people will come in – from General Motors to the Japanese to the Koreans?

And if we all took the advice of the economists that we shouldn't bend down to pick up £50 notes, surely there *would* be some £50 notes left lying on the pavement?

It's a fair point.

The answer is that there *are* obviously some opportunities to make profit, and there are occasional £50 notes lying around. But the key to finding them without wasting a lot of effort in the process is *information*; information that has value and that others might not have. If you know where a £50 was dropped, you might be in a good position to find it.

And in business, it is possible to competition-proof a good idea. But when you do, it will come from holding information.

The stuff that you know about entering a market which your competitors don't.

This is an important issue for entrepreneurs. It's what made Ford and IKEA. Acquiring useful information, using it wisely and building on it step by step are things that successful companies do.

VALUE AND INFORMATION

There are two things to say about information. The first is that it can be valuable because business is inherently very unpredictable. It's a game of chance. Some things that shouldn't sell do; some things that should sell don't. No amount of good business acumen can substitute for real market intelligence.

Think of the mobile-phone companies discovering that what their customers liked was plain old text messaging, far more than all the extravagant (and expensive) features like WAP access to the internet.

Given that business works this way, good strategy is not just about designing and selling your product. It's also about acquiring information as to what works and what doesn't. In fact, often the *information* you hold is as valuable as your product.

So even if you have an idea that anyone can copy, you might have enough specific information about running that business to give yourself a lead over your rivals.

I'm not talking about the kind of information you can look up in the library (the size of the garden-rake market in the different countries of the European Union, for example, because your competitors can look that up too).

No, the valuable information tells you what sells; what the customers seem to like about the product or are willing to pay for it; what they find most annoying about the product, or don't understand in the instruction manual; what problems crop up in production; which bits of the device break first.

All these things you discover on the job, and they are all very valuable.

And they can allow companies to exploit their good ideas without having their profits driven away by intense competition. Entrepreneurs who acquire information by being first, or at least early into the market, have a head start over their competitors that might allow them to make serious money before anyone else catches up. Even if the good times won't last forever, they might last long enough to buy them a nice pension.

So if you are pitching to the Dragons, and you are looking for a convincing answer to general questions about how you intend to competition-proof your idea, your answer might be that you have an early lead in the market.

And to make *that* compelling, you had better show that having a head start over your competitors is valuable.

In selling a piece of furniture that looks after our half-dirty clothes, an early lead is probably not particularly important. The product is not very difficult to produce or sell, and so the information you have may not be worth very much.

But if your product is a complex one, and if you have learned a lot on the way to producing it, you might be able to get established in business fast enough to make big profits for some period before others catch up.

Or even better, you might find an IKEA who wants to buy you out rather than copy you. For them it can make sense, as it might be cheaper than re-inventing what you've done. And even if they don't pay a very high price, it does provide a return on the work you've done and the idea you've had.

However, there is a second important point about information.

It's the key to minimising the risks you take with your investors' money. If your new business is a gamble, then by far the most useful thing you can do is try to provide better information about the odds. There's no point in pretending or acting as though success is assured.

At each stage of the life of your business, only invest what you need to learn to decide whether it's worth proceeding to the next stage.

For example, if you want to be Henry Ford and you want to build cars, don't start by building a huge factory. That risks a lot of money before you have any information about the market. Try, instead, to build a few cars and see how they go down. Launch in one small market first – you will know pretty quickly whether it's worth launching elsewhere.

Clever management involves sequencing your decisions in order to minimise the commitments you make, while maximising the information you obtain.

In fact, you may be able to ascertain very quickly whether a business is likely to fly for a relatively small amount of money. That can save you pitching for an investment of a large amount, and it might allow you to keep a far higher proportion of your company than if you attempt to go big straightaway, risking a lot of other people's capital in the process.

One final detail: there is no point in devoting much effort to obtaining information if you don't act upon it.

So the downside of obtaining intelligence about the market is that it may be the death knell of your company. It may tell you to give up rather than carry on.

Frequently, there are people who can't take 'no' for an answer from the information that comes in. Some think that if they can just try again, it'll turn out well. Which may of course be true. It's just that it's very risky to keep trying. If you want to persuade an investor to help you take such a risk, you'll probably have to give them most of the company.

Often, it's not even worth having another go.

Devastating as this is, it is generally better to give up before you have burned through a mortgage on your house, and several hundred thousand pounds of investors' money.

Many entrepreneurs fail to see that. It's very difficult when you are so close to a business, and so much of the meaning of your life is tied into it.

That's where the Dragons' difficult questions are useful. They get you to think about the value you have, the way you shield it from competition, and the information you have to help you in that goal.

For good or bad, though, if you pitch to the Dragons and your answers to their questions are poor, you can expect them to tell you.

GETTING THE
NUMBERS RIGHT

This is the chapter you need to read twice. Few new businesses can succeed without a bit of planning and some clear thinking about costs and sales, or what Evan calls 'the numbers'. Here, he gives an introduction to the most important concepts, and his guide as to how you should use them.

You don't have to watch *Dragons' Den* very carefully to notice that a lot of people get into a tangle with their numbers.

It would be tempting to think that the Dragons use numbers as some kind of ritual torture, but in fact, understanding a few key numbers about a business is much the same as understanding the business itself. You may not find the numbers come easily, and you may find you lose your memory of them under pressure. That's fine. You are not looking for a job as a financial analyst, or a mathematician.

However, you still need to be able to translate your understanding of what your company will achieve into the language of numbers, just as an estate agent needs to be able to talk about a property using numbers to describe the price and the area of land it covers.

There's no need to get too cut up about it. When making a pitch and when setting out your goals for the business, you don't have to be too precise – you are not filling out a tax return (that comes later) – all you must do is work out a rough guide to revenues and costs for the next few years of your business's life.

Of course, things won't work exactly to plan and it would be silly to assume they will, but there are still several good reasons to produce your cost and revenue estimates.

First, you're testing whether your business is viable at all (if costs exceed revenues indefinitely, your business is probably not viable, although that didn't discourage lots of internet start-ups in the late 1990s).

Second, you're estimating the value of your company. Once you have mapped out a reasonable projection of revenues and costs, you can forecast your profits, and once you have a profits figure, you have a good idea of how much an investor might pay for shares now, and how much an investor might reap from your business on exiting it in a few years' time.

Third, if you are reasonably sophisticated about it, the revenue and cost figures will tell you about cash flow. They will tell whether – even if your business is viable and valuable – there will be some periods when cash will run out and you'll need funds to tide you over.

Finally, producing revenue and cost projections is a great discipline. It will give you some realistic expectations of your business and it will alert you to all sorts of questions about where the key unknowns lie.

Perhaps it's best not to look at your financial projections as a forecast, but as a reality check. They force you to make some assumptions about the different uncertainties you inevitably face (just how many widgets can you sell next year?) and to ensure that your assumptions apply consistently (if you think you will sell 50,000 widgets, you had better allow costs to cover the manufacture of 50,000 widgets, not 30,000).

Having made some consistent assumptions, you can check whether you are on track to meet your goals, and you can see what exactly you need to achieve to at least break even. You can stare your assumptions in the face, and ask yourself whether people really will pay that much for what you are selling, or whether they really will buy that quantity.

All in all, whether the Dragons want numbers or not, *you* should want to produce some kind of financial projections for your own management purposes.

So let's see how you go about it.

AN EASY EXAMPLE

In principle, all you need are two things: your costs and revenues. Fixate on those. Everything depends on the latter ultimately exceeding the former.

In practice, a bit of science and quite a bit of art are involved in sorting that out. Proper financial planning is quite complicated and it's best to get help from someone who knows what they are doing or at least to use one of the financial-planning templates that you can download from the web to guide you. They'll ensure you treat important issues like VAT properly.

Life is particularly hard for established companies, which start out with creditors, debtors, stock and work in progress that make the projections more complicated. They have to plan properly.

But even if you need help with the full works, the rudimentary basics of your business are things *you* should understand – and in truth, it is those basics which will interest intelligent investors.

It helps enormously if you have the ability to play with a spreadsheet – mainly because that does all the calculating for you, it looks nice and clear and you can change things very easily. If you have never used one, it is not a bad idea to learn. But whether you do it on a spreadsheet, on downloadable software, on paper or with beads on an abacus, the task is roughly the same.

At its simplest, imagine you are setting up a hypothetical business that will sell 'widgets', you need to know or make assumptions about:

- The *Direct cost* to you, of making or buying each widget
- The *Price* at which you can sell each widget
- The *Number* of widgets you expect to sell
- The *Overhead* cost of running the office, rent, marketing and paying yourself a salary (yes, you should factor your own time into the costs of the business, even if you don't actually pay yourself a salary in practice).

Then, using your best guesses on each of these four things, you can calculate the important numbers for each of the next few years. First, is your **total revenue**:

Total revenue = Price times Number sold

And then you find your **Total cost of sales**:

Total cost of sales = Direct cost times Number sold

From which you can work out your **Gross profit** – i.e. your Profit before Overheads

Gross profit = Total revenue minus Total cost of sales

And then your **Net profit** – i.e. your Gross Profit after Overheads

Net profit = Gross profit minus Overheads

(At this Net profit stage of the calculation, you should also subtract any interest you think you might need to pay on debts you've taken out.)

Do that for each of the next five years (now you see why it helps to have a spreadsheet) and you are well on your way.

You can also use this to work out the key ratios – your **Mark-up** and your **Margin**.

Mark-up = Gross profit divided by Direct cost of sales (multiplied by 100, to turn it into a percentage)

Gross margin = Gross profit divided by Total revenue

Net margin = Net profit divided by Total revenue (again, both multiplied by 100, to turn them into a percentage)

Now you can play with your data to work out all sorts of interesting things. For example, ask yourself at what level of Costs does my Net profit disappear? How low does my price go before my Net profit disappears?

These are not funny numbers for accountants to file away; these are things that need to be at the front of your mind. Every day in business you will be getting market intelligence – learning what sells; what price turns customers away; what costs you can achieve with bulk orders – and every day you need to benchmark the information you get in against the key numbers thrown up by your financial projections.

The numbers also tell you where your business is vulnerable, and where you most need extra information before you proceed further.

But the great news is that even with very simple financial modelling, you probably have enough information to answer 90 per cent of the difficult number questions the Dragons are likely to ask you about your business.

Phew. No need to get in a tangle.

Alas, that's not the end of the challenge.

TESTING YOUR ASSUMPTIONS

Just because you have the numbers, it doesn't mean you have the answers to all the difficult questions about your business. Those normally come down to the assumptions you have made in deriving your numbers.

So before you pitch, and before you embark on selling a single widget, you need to look at your assumptions. One by one, you need to question them, bend them, break them and re-make them. This is the fundamental sanity check that any new business needs to engage in.

There is a pretty recurring mistake made by entrepreneurs – one might call it the *Dragons' Den* delusion because it particularly seems to afflict those who walk up the stairs to face the Dragons. It is the mistake of succumbing to over-optimism, of putting more weight on positive evidence than negative and of failing to spot the potential for things to go wrong.

To avoid this, an open mind and solid market research are most useful. By looking at what other similar companies have achieved, you are more likely to make realistic estimates of your own prospects.

Armed with these, you should think about all your assumptions on price, volume and cost. We can look at each of these in turn.

PRICE

You have two prices to think about. The one at which you sell the product, and the (probably higher) price at which the consumer buys it. After all, in many businesses there's often a distribution chain that needs a pretty big margin to carry your product. So you need to test both prices against the best evidence you can find.

For a simple manufactured good, a rule of thumb is that the retail price is about three or four times the price at which you make it or buy it in. It may be more, it can be less, depending on the precise sector and kind of retailin. But you should ensure that you are making realistic assumptions about the retailer and everybody else's profit, as well as your own.

You might, for example, assume you will buy your widget from a Chinese manufacturer at £1, then you sell it at £2 to a retailer who sells it at £4.

Once you have made an assumption about a retail price, and derived your own sale price accordingly, you also have to think about how realistic it is for consumers to want to pay that retail price for your product. This is not easy to uncover.

There's no point in *asking* people directly if they will pay a certain price for your item. They will often say 'yes' to the abstract question just to please, especially if you have a look of forlorn hope in your eyes, and it's not what people say that matters. It's whether they will part with their cash on the day.

So the best thing to do is look at what they pay for similar products now. That's where market research comes in. If you're selling widgets, what other widgets are available and at what price do they sell?

Your product might be better than similar products on the market – which means yours might expect to sell at a higher price. But at least test your assumption about your price by comparing it to the version already available.

If your widget lasts twice as long as other widgets, it will sell for more than other widgets – but probably not for more than twice the price. If your widget is also able to double up as a garden rake, it is unlikely people will pay more for your widget than it costs them to buy an old style widget *and* a garden rake. By looking at the existing market, and how consumers behave in it, you can obtain realistic limits on the price that you can get away with.

Once you have come up with a price assumption, you can test how sensitive your business is to the price. For example, try to ensure your business is still viable, even if you are wrong on price by a big margin.

VOLUMES

Next, you need to investigate any assumptions you make about the volume you will sell. It's easy to succumb to the old *Dragons' Den* delusions on sales. You can make assumptions which sound fine, but which are, in practice, way off the mark.

For example, you might imagine yourself renting a space in a trade fair at which, you have been told, 100,000 people will attend. It's easy to think to yourself, 'If only one in 100 of those people stop to look at my widgets, and then only one in 25 of those people actually buy it, I'll still sell 10 widgets, which would be a good day's work.'

In practice, it could easily be one in a thousand who stop to talk to you, and half of them will just want to know the way to the toilets.

So, guessing your sales in advance from a standing start is extremely difficult. It's impossible to ensure that your hope is not prevailing over your judgement

By far the best way of estimating sales is to have some real evidence of real buyers actually parting with real cash for your product.

If you have some early stock, try selling it at a trade fair. Or try getting some into one local shop on a trial basis. If you are offering a service, try getting some buyers. You don't really need money from these prototype sales – as the last chapter explained, you want something far more valuable, information about your market.

If the product sells well in one shop, you are in good shape. It's a sign. Just as an opinion poll of a thousand people can be a good indication of how 30 million people will vote, one shop is far better evidence than none.

If your product doesn't sell, think hard. If it hasn't sold, it might be that the customers haven't properly understood the genius of your design and need more time to grasp it, but more likely, it means that your product isn't much in demand.

What you should not do is make the classic error of assuming that if you sell one widget in one test shop, you can potentially sell ten thousand widgets if you can get them into ten thousand shops. On that logic, you can sell a million if you can get in to all the shops in the world. The problem is, if you only sell one per shop, no shops will bother to stock it and you won't sell any at all. You can't reduce your failure by trying to scale it up.

However, if your product does sell well in one test market, then you can research the number of shops out there, to derive estimates of the total market potential for your product.

Similar arguments apply to you, if you are selling a service. Test your sales, and only if the test succeeds, think about the scale of the market.

If you do not have any trial data on which to base your estimates of sales, what do you do? Answer: you base estimates on the sales of your closest competitors. If you are selling a new kind of rake, you look at the market for rakes and the sales of different rake makers, and you estimate how far you might go in matching them.

Notice that I said you need to look at your *closest* competitors. If you are selling rakes, you look at rake sales; you don't benchmark your sales estimates against the entire market for garden tools. Define your industry narrowly, and make estimates accordingly.

Once you have some estimates of sales, whether you get them from real data, or from realistic estimates, you need to do some basic checks against them.

Have an argument with yourself. Play devil's advocate, arguing against your estimates, and ask yourself some difficult questions about what your sales figures imply:

- If I meet these sales figures, what proportion of the total market am I taking?
- Where would my sales leave me, relative to the current market leader?
- If I achieve my sales, how many homes will have my product after five years?

If you find that your assumptions imply that, in five years, you have sold more than the entire population of the known universe could want, then you have been too optimistic. Indeed, if you can't spot some vulnerabilities in your assumptions, you probably haven't subjected them to sufficient criticism, and if *you* don't criticise them, a potential investor probably will.

COSTS

Finally, there are costs. You will probably estimate these before you even think about price and volumes. And you will probably have a better idea of wage levels or manufacturing costs than you do of consumer demand. If you don't, you can obtain a good idea by getting contractors to quote for you.

Just as with prices and volumes though, it is easy to succumb to *Dragons' Den* delusions and to be too optimistic about how easy things are.

First, you will probably underestimate your overheads – running an office is more expensive and more work than it seems.

Second, it is easy to overlook the costs of unforeseen events. Some of your production may go wrong: you will have to fix it. You may offer guarantees which can't be ignored – they are a significant liability.

The occasional costs of dealing with misfortunes have to be factored into the average cost of everyday production.

Finally, it is easy to think you can get things for free which you will have to pay for if your business is to be called successful. You might get your friend to do your book-keeping at the moment in return for a bottle of something. You can't assume he will still do it for you when you become a multinational firm.

You can't even assume that your time is free. You might offer it up for nothing in the start-up phase – it will almost certainly make perfect sense to – but in working out the long-term economics of your product, you have to factor in all costs, and the fact that you are working (and hence are not available to earn a salary elsewhere) is a cost.

SCALING UP THE BUSINESS

The dream of many investors is to identify businesses that can be scaled up, so that an initial success grows to be success time ten or a hundred.

In the easy example of a widget maker, it's straightforward to take ball-park estimates of the cost, the selling price and the profit made on each widget, to see how profitable your business is as you scale up the size of your business.

Tell me how much profit you make selling 100 widgets through one shop, and I can make a simple guess that you'll be 50 times more profitable if you sell 5,000 widgets through 50 shops.

Such easily calculable rules of thumb are very useful to you and your investors in working out how much potential upside (and downside) there is from your business.

Unfortunately, the calculation of scale is complicated for companies whose output is not so easily counted into discrete units like widgets.

An optician might make money from selling glasses and providing eye tests; a shop will have lots of different products on sale; a theatre school will have different classes of different sizes.

Obviously, if you have a complicated business with multiple revenues you can think of it as a lot of smaller businesses, each with one product. That's a perfectly sensible approach. And in a spreadsheet of costs and revenues you may model your different activities that way.

But in reality, your different products are probably related. The optician finds the more eye tests she does, the more glasses she can sell. It doesn't make sense to think of scaling up the eye-tests business, without thinking about scaling up the sales of glasses.

It's also true for most businesses – they produce several things at the same time and sales of one item affect sales of the others. Costs of one item can also have a bearing on the costs of several of the other items produced. They are not really separate businesses at all.

So you have to ask yourself, 'If I was to scale up the size of my business, how would I scale it up?'

If you sell teddy bears with a built-in video player, then the revenues you make from the teddy-bear sales will affect the revenues you can make from selling videos. So you would aim to sell more bears, and as a result more videos too.

If you understand your business, you should also have a good idea of the relationship between the revenues and costs of video sales and teddy-bear sales.

More generally, if you want to think about scaling up your business you should think about the costs and revenues associated with increasing your main output, and then also think about the implications of increasing the other related outputs by the same proportion.

VALUING THE BUSINESS

Suppose you have covered the basics. You understand the complexities of your business; you've tested your assumptions and are on solid ground. You've got a well-grounded financial model that projects solid net profits for the next five years.

Now you are ready for a discussion with potential investors about the value of your company.

This might be nasty, so only read this section after the watershed.

I'm afraid I have to tell you that the value of your business today – *before* it has delivered the net profit promised in the financial projections – is only a fraction of what it will be worth *after* it has delivered the net profit. Sorry about that.

I know that you think nothing can go wrong now and you're assuming that estimated profit will be made, and hence assuming your embryonic business is worth a lot right now. But it ain't so.

It is the biggest *Dragons' Den* delusion of all and one of the most common mistakes entrepreneurs make. They fail to see that a business is like a lottery ticket. The ones we know are winners *after* the draw are worth a whole lot more than the ones we hold before the lottery balls have been plucked.

Even if you can't imagine how the business could fail, even when you have built in pessimistic assumptions galore, be prepared for today's value to reflect the significant risk that your business won't take off at all.

Now, this recognition has generally been in short supply in discussions about value in *Dragons' Den*, which seem to have evolved as follows: entrepreneurs have observed that the Dragons drive a hard bargain and typically take two or three times as much of the company as was originally offered. So entrepreneurs offer smaller and smaller proportions of their business, on the apparently unarguable logic that if the Dragons are going to triple the starting offer then it's better they triple a small offer of shares, rather than a big one.

I don't think it works like that.

There may be some tactical benefits to pitching your shares at a very high price.

Personally, though, I doubt it.

I think it's better to demand a realistic price for your shares, probably erring significantly on the high side, but not so high as to be on a different planet.

Imagine yourself selling a £200,000 house. You might reasonably put it on the market for £250,000, but not £800,000. If you did, you would still find a buyer, but you wouldn't get £400,000 for it, and you would get laughed at for being someone who doesn't know the value of a house.

Obviously, if you do go into the Den pitching realistically, you have less room to yield concessions in any negotiation. So be it. You'll have to be tough, and not move very far. But that is still better than starting with an offer of 5 per cent of the equity, and then jumping to 20 per cent in the first move.

Now the reason people get into a pickle on valuation is that they think it is just a matter of negotiation and attitude and, they surmise, there's no science to it so there's no basis for doing anything other than to make up numbers that suit them.

Which is what they then do.

However, there is a little bit of science to it, and you should understand it.

STEP ONE:
THE FUTURE VALUE OF THE BUSINESS

For a new business with only a small track record, the first thing to have in mind is the value of the business in three to five years' time, if and when the business plan is achieved – that's when much of the launch risk has been resolved satisfactorily and when you or your investors might want to sell out.

At that stage your company should be worth something in the order of five to ten times the net profit for that year. Call it ten for simplicity. If it expects to make £200,000 profit in five years, it will then be worth about £2 million in five years.

It won't be exactly ten times profits. The value might be higher than £2 million if you are lucky and the net profit is still growing fast. Even more likely, it will be worth less. And anyway, you should subtract tax from the net profit before multiplying it up. You must also think about the company's assets and its debts, as well as the risks and sustainability of the profits generated.

But think in terms of ten times profit as a ball park.

What drives that 'ten' is the economy and interest rates and all that business. In five years' time, investors with £2 million pounds could invest in a savings account and earn, say, 5 per cent free of any risk at all, i.e. they could make £100,000 a year in the bank. To be induced to invest in your company in five years' time, they need to expect to do better than that. So, we tend to assume they'll probably require a return of about £200,000 of business profits, to compensate them for not taking the guaranteed £100,000 they could make from putting their money in the bank.

STEP TWO:
THE VALUE TODAY

So far, we've been discussing the value of the company after it has delivered the business plan – that's all about the value in three to five years' time.

When you are in the Den, it's the value today that matters, and in general, there's another rule of thumb – also involving the number ten – to calculate the value today. Think of the value of your company now as being about a tenth of its value in five years.

For example, if your company projects a net profit of £200,000 in five years' time, making it worth about £2 million in the future, divide the value by ten to get to an estimate of a reasonable value now. So, it's worth about £200,000 today.

You'll notice that the two rules of thumb kind of cancel out –

the value of a company today is about one-tenth of a number that is ten times the expected profit in five years. So speaking very roughly, the value today is likely to have a similar order of magnitude to the expected profit in three to five years' time.

You can argue around these figures – there are those who think that one or other of the 'tens' should be five or fifteen – there is room for as much argument as there is in the value of a house.

Certainly, for an existing business with a track record of delivering profits, you would not expect the risk to be so high, and the Dragons would not necessarily need to see their investment grow nearly so far.

But while it is not very exact, there is a ball park to play in.

VALUING A SHARE

Valuing a company is important. But in *Dragons' Den*, there is less talk about the value of the whole entity, and more talk about the share that the Dragons should get for their investment.

As it happens, knowing the proportion of the company the Dragons want for £100,000 is just a short piece of mental arithmetic away from knowing the value they put on the company as a whole. If you should find yourself negotiating with the Dragons, you need to be able to flip between your valuation, their valuation and the specific proportion of the company their money buys. And you should be able to do so with ease.

Most entrepreneurs understand the basics of percentages – but you can never assume anything. So it is worth reiterating here, despite the risk of insulting many readers' abilities.

To get from a percentage of a number to a proportion of it, simply divide the percentage by 100. For example, 10 per cent of a number is equal to 0.1 times that number.

If a company is worth £100,000, then 10 per cent of the company is worth 0.1 times £100,000 (which is £10,000).

Equally, if the Dragons say £10,000 should buy 10 per cent of a company, then the implied value of the whole company is £10,000 *divided by* 0.1 (which is £100,000).

There is an obvious complication, though.

When investors put money into a company, they are usually not buying shares from someone who wants to sell them. They are buying shares of a company so that the money goes into the company to help it expand.

So if you agree with the Dragons that your business is worth £100,000 before the Dragons invest in it, and the Dragons invest £50,000, it should be worth £150,000 after the investment (and the Dragons should get a third of the post-investment business).

As the only point of any negotiation is to divide a share in the event of an investment occurring, so you should always think of the value of the company post-investment, and you should negotiate on that basis.

But when you walk into the Den, or any other investment pitch, it is worth you knowing what value you are putting on your business both post- and pre-investment. It's quite simple to flip between the two. If you are asking for £50,000 and are offering a 20 per cent share, you are suggesting that the business will be worth £250,000 once the investment has been paid in. And as £50,000 is being paid in, that implies the business is worth £250,000 minus £50,000 before the investment has been paid.

It can be painful to write these things out, but for most investors, the calculations are pure instinct. The first thing the Dragons do on hearing a pitch is to make the mental calculation as to the value of the company implied by your offer. Indeed, some of them can't really think about the pitch without thinking about the value of the company they are buying into.

And generally, they find that people have valued their companies far too generously.

This is sometimes controversial. Some people believe the Dragons are far too mean, in taking large stakes of companies, for mere tens of thousands of pounds, implicitly putting a low value on the companies.

So do the Dragons take too big a cut?

It's true, they can do very well. The price they pay implies they can perhaps expect to make about a ten-fold return on their investment over the next few years if all goes to plan.

A *ten-fold return* you say. That sounds like a lot more than they would get in a savings account.

But not everything does go to plan, generally speaking.

If nine out of ten great businesses fail to deliver what's promised, investors need to score really big on the remaining one that does succeed.

Their job is to pick the winners. Your job is to make sure you are among them.

And that means you shouldn't become a slave to the numbers you produce and you shouldn't spend all your time gazing at spreadsheets or valuing the business you have created.

No, your job is to understand your business using numbers where that helps. And to spend most of your day making a business that beats the numbers you're working with.

If you think the investors are unduly mean, if you think that you could pick a successful business with a better hit rate, and that you would pay a higher price for early-stage investments, then you should probably not be pitching to the Dragons – you should be a venture capitalist.

PART 4
INSIDE THE DEN
SERIES 5

The Dragons are challenging characters and as rivals in the Den they test each other almost as much as they test the entrepreneurs. James was the new face in the Den in series five. He was subject to teasing – off-screen they called him a 'new boy' and joked about his sartorial style and his love of cars – but he soon proved he could hold his own, especially when he made the best investment of the series, which is one of the case studies that follows.

They may each be very different characters, but what all the Dragons have in common is the ability to spot a good deal a mile off. They all drive a hard bargain but as well as making money, they are clearly having fun. These case studies cannot cover all the laughs in the series and everyone will have their favourite moments. Andy Harmer's Double Date pitch went badly wrong – his David Beckham character found it hard to speak, but then he brought on his Captain Jack Sparrow and Will Smith look-alikes and the Dragons were lost for words. Shaun Tulfrey accused Deborah of having highlights in her hair.

Deborah was right to be rather miffed – she's a purely natural blond! You may also remember how Theo and Deborah invested in Max McModo's extraordinary Restore furniture range, which is now a major feature of Theo's office.

The special Dragons' Den *programme for* Children in Need *was a particular success as it was viewed by 9.5 million people. The programme normally has to turn away the many 14 and 15 year olds who are too young to appear in the Den, but for* Children in Need, *young entrepreneurs were called in to pitch to the Dragons. James Caan invested £5,000 in a nine year old called James who had an anti-bullying campaign that he wanted to launch called 'Look for Loneliness'. Although he was the youngest ever contender on the show young James received two offers from the Dragons. Duncan offered to split the deal with James Caan but young James said 'No, I want to go with big James.' At the end of the programme Duncan asked him why and young James replied 'because he's a new Dragon and I didn't want him to be lonely.'*

There is no set formula in succeeding to get on the show. In the next section you will read how Peter Moule demonstrated his electrician's Chocbox to the production team after he'd had a few drinks at an exhibition centre. Laban Roomes should have appeared on earlier programmes but kept dropping out as he kept changing his mind about whether he was ready to put himself on the line. There doesn't seem to be a clear process for being a success once you're on the show, either, as the variety of case studies put forward by the Dragons demonstrate.

In Peter Jones' case study, 'A Lesson in Seeing the Bigger Picture', the Dragon invests in one of the brightest people to appear on the show. It is clear that Peter loves the idea of helping children do better as school, and is excited by Mark Champkin's inventions which aid concentration. The case study demonstrates the winning combination of Mark doing what he does best – coming up with new ideas and designing – and Peter doing what he does best – getting stuff on shelves and back off them and through the tills.

Deborah Meaden's case study is 'A Lesson in Creativity'. She saw the opportunity to make money in the Youdoodoll, but also to have some fun working with Sarah Lu. The combination of Sarah Lu's creativity and Deborah's mentoring the slightly tougher business side is a winner.

Theo Paphitis's case study is 'A Lesson in Making The Web Work for You', although perhaps it is also a lesson about Theo's family values – the fact that Mrs P plays on-line bingo had alerted him to the enormous potential of the market. Theo wanted to make Emmie Matthews and Ed Stevens of Gaming Alert part of his business family and now they are working from his office. His commitment of £200,000 as a single investment was one of the largest offered in the Den and is testimony to the huge potential that Theo could see in the market. Who would have thought that Theo would know about bingo? The Dragons have enormous business experience outside the Den and they surprise the entrepreneurs by suddenly revealing themselves as expert in areas we did not know about.

Duncan Bannatyne's case study on Peter Moule's Chocbox offers 'A Lesson in Exploiting The Market'. If you have seen the show you will remember that this is the one of the rare occasions when Deborah makes *a mistake. She said, 'If it looks too good to be true, I usually think it is too good to be true.' But she was wrong! In a unique deal moment, Peter Moule was honest that what he needed was the expertise of the Dragons, not their money. The* Dragons' Den *production team think that this episode was the sign of a mature series: 'Obviously the investment was important to Peter – but more than that, and priceless to him in progressing his business, was the input of the Dragons because he wanted to take his business global and he wanted to take it retail.'*

James Caan has two case studies: 'A Lesson in Cash Flow' and 'A Lesson in Building Business Around An Individual'. In the series James showed that he was quite prepared to try things out. The production team 'don't want someone in there who just sits back and watches' but they also saw that he was 'considerate and people focused'. James invested in Laban Roomes' gold-plating business, and saw beyond the business to the entrepreneur behind. It's a particular trait of James that he concentrates on the individual as he does both with Laban and with Sammy with her Fit-Fur-Life business.

The following case studies will explore what ticks the boxes for the Dragons and inspire you to start your own business.

A LESSON IN SEEING THE BIGGER PICTURE:
MARK CHAMPKINS' CONCENTRATE

If you're 2 per cent dehydrated your concentration drops by 20 per cent (World Bank). This is one of the facts that inspired serial inventor Mark Champkins to design a new range of products that help children concentrate so that they get the most out of their time at school. When he arrived in the Den he was already selling his Concentrate products in the Science Museum, in the Design Museum, on johnlewis.com and in the John Lewis store on Oxford Street, London.

Mark studied manufacturing and engineering at Cambridge University followed by an MA in product design at the Royal College of Art so his educational background is a perfect mix of the logical thinking required for manufacturing and the lateral creative thinking used in product design.

A winner of British Inventor of the Year (2002) for his self-heating crockery, Mark has always had a passion for invention. As a child, his best invention was peg guns – he took a clothes peg apart and using elastic bands and the metal part of the pegs as 'bullets' Mark and his three rumbustious brothers would fight dangerous peg-gun wars! Encouraged by their father, the brothers became go-kart builders making three-wheelers, six-wheelers and one with a roll-bar and a light on the front for racing in the dark.

As the first member of his family to go to university Mark has always been interested in education and was excited to be sponsored by MAK architects to investigate new classroom design. He realised that although a lot of government money was being spent on fantastic new buildings, often the absolute essentials for learning were being overlooked. 'It doesn't matter how futuristic the classroom looks if the results aren't practical and ignore the needs of the children. You have to engage children's attention, and make sure that they're in the right state to learn.'

Working with teachers he looked at factors that affect children's concentration such as dehydration and uncomfortable furniture, and after a year of research he had designed five products to remind children to drink water, to make chairs more comfortable, and to encourage healthy eating and exercise.

With investment from NESTA (National Endowment Society of Technology in the Arts) he produced a business plan and was given funding to get his ideas into production, sourcing a manufacturer in China. His products were on sale but how could he build his business?

Needing both advice and investment, he decided to try *Dragons' Den*.

After a straightforward audition Mark set off to the Den to pitch to the Dragons. 'Waiting was like being at the dentist. It got really difficult because I had to be on permanent standby, and obviously I was trying to keep as sharp and focused as I could, but it was six hours before I got called in. I walked up the steps and tried to calm down but before I knew it I was in the middle of the pitch. I was answering questions and I suddenly caught myself thinking "I can't believe this has happened so quickly".'

Mark was impressed by the Dragons because they seemed genuinely interested in his ideas. He had a range of Concentrate products to show them: a school bag that hooks over a chair to make it more comfortable; a cooler jacket for a water bottle that's also a pen holder so that the bottle can be kept on the desk to prompt the child to drink more water; and the lunchbox and lunchbox cooler bag that encourage healthy eating.

Then he asked for £100,000 in return for a 15 per cent share of his business. But although the Dragons were interested in education, they were not enthusiastic about the business opportunity. After James, Deborah and Duncan dropped out retail expert Theo Paphitis said:

'I think you've got some good thoughts, but you need to get some commercial ideas if you're going to make money. So I'm out.'

Peter Jones, however, held a different view:

'I was impressed when I saw the product and I got the vision straight away. I've got five kids, and I thought, "My children would love that." So I was thinking about the opportunity while the other Dragons were busy telling Mark why his ideas wouldn't work and then I was able to pounce.'

With the other four Dragons out, Peter revealed his hand.

Mark says, 'He told me afterwards he was interested from the outset, but stayed very quiet and was waiting for the other Dragons to drop out and was quite pleased when they did.'

But Peter's offer was for more than just the business:

'I'm really interested and I'm going to make you an offer, but it is contingent on you putting all of your inventions into one company.'

Then the bargaining began. Peter offered the full £100,000 but he wanted a hefty 40 per cent stake in Mark's company and all of Mark's future inventions. Mark was only prepared to give him 30 per cent. Neither side wanted to back down. Sometimes in the Den more happens than there is time to show on the programme, and in Mark's case, some tough negotiation took place.

Mark said that Theo was particularly kind and offered him a job: 'Look, if nobody makes you an offer, I'd be happy to take you on as a designer if you wanted.' Theo's interest helped Mark during the negotiation. Mark admits he was a bit cheeky with his future business partner saying, 'Listen to Theo, he knows what he's doing, why not listen to his advice.' So a compromise was reached – Peter's final offer was 40 per cent but if Mark made a £250,000 profit in three years then Peter would give him back 5 per cent of the business. As Mark was forecasting an even higher profit margin, he agreed.

Mark was elated. He thought that Peter, of all the Dragons, could bring the most to the business. After he left the Den he met Peter's team: 'It was very interesting to look at the different aspects of his business and see where he was based and how he ran things.

When you look at some of the other things he's invested in like Reggae Reggae Sauce and the iTeddy you can't help but think, "Well that's it, I've got it made!"'

More important, Mark believes that Peter can involve himself at a high level – making introductions and looking through the presentations and the pitches, using his expertise to guide the direction of the company. Mark has had the opportunity to do more design work and develop new ideas with schools. On the commercial front, John Lewis Partnership is rolling out Concentrate to all their stores, and Lakeland is also selling his products. Peter talks to Mark every week and his team are very supportive so Mark is confident that the business can only get better.

And Peter has great faith in the expanding product range:

'Mark's a true inventor with a vision to deliver ideas that enhance the quality of life. 2008 is going to be a great year for all his product range in major stores.'

A LESSON IN CREATIVITY:
SARAH LU AND YOUDOO DOLL

Sarah Lu appeared in the Den with her Youdoo Doll, a rag doll that can be given the computerised face of its owner and dressed to suit the owner's whim. Creative, energetic Sarah had already sold her idea to Topshop and to three novelty web sites, but the dolls were still being made at home by her 'auntie, family and friends.' Sarah hoped the Dragons would help her expand the fledgling business and develop the brand. She expected Theo to be the one to take the bait, but her strongest supporter turned out to be Deborah.

Sarah Lu's story is all about making something from nothing. Her parents were Vietnamese boat people who arrived in Britain in 1979 with no possessions. Sarah was born in a refugee camp in Lincolnshire; her 20-year-old mother spoke no English.

Times were hard, but with her natural talents, her ambition, and the support of her extended family, Sarah made rapid progress towards her goal of starting her own business. As Deborah Meaden spotted right away, Sarah had always been creative: 'That was obvious from the minute the top of her head started appearing, as she came up the stairs.' As a child, Sarah had loved programmes like *Blue Peter* which showed how to make things, and from aged ten she knew she wanted a career in graphic design. She always gave handmade Christmas and birthday presents. 'I was a low-tech person; I've always used recycled stuff, whatever was around me.'

Her family weren't sure about an art-based career. They wanted her to play safe with a professional career such as accountancy. But Sarah was determined to show them that creativity could also bring financial rewards – 'Success can be about doing what you love.' Deborah Meaden sympathises; 'The key with Sarah Lu is to keep her in the creative zone. I don't need Sarah to be doing accounts and packing up boxes, her time should be freed up to do what she does best.'

Instead of A-levels, Sarah did a BTEC course in graphics followed by a degree in graphic design and illustration. She had grown up in Northampton, but with characteristic independence she moved to Brighton at the age of 20 just because she liked the idea of it. Looking for help in building up her graphic design company, she joined Sussex Enterprise. Alongside her desire to forge a career out of her creativity she had another ambition, to buy her mother a house. 'And I'd also like to buy myself a helicopter!'

She had had the idea for Youdoo Dolls for a long time. A few years ago she entered it for a competition, and though she didn't win she 'nearly got there.' Sure that her business idea was a good one, but less sure that she'd ever find a backer, she 'ran a pub for a couple of years as my own franchise.' She saved hard; after two years she had £6,000, and spent the whole lot on 1,000 dolls. 'It literally went in one second. But I thought, if I don't put my money where my mouth is, who is going to? It was the greatest risk I ever took.'

With 1,000 dolls sitting in her bedroom waiting for action, Sarah wasn't sure where to turn next. 'Then I thought about a trade show I'd heard of through Sussex Enterprise.' Sarah's boyfriend ran up a credit-card debt to lend her the £2,500 she needed for her stand at the trade show; she sold nearly all her stock in three days. The principal buyers were Top Shop, iwantoneofthese.com, needapresent.com and gadgets.co.uk.

Despite this success, Sarah was still penniless. Her profits from the trade show went on paying off debts. She knew that unless her buyers put in a second order her bank would not back her. Then Christine, her mentor at Sussex Enterprise, suggested that she apply for *Dragons' Den*.

'Christine's the most amazing woman I've ever met in my life, apart from my mum. She's helped me the whole way. So I took her advice and applied online for the Den, and the next day I had a phone call saying, "We'd like you to come in for a meeting with us."' Sarah had ideas for at least six products, but she decided to concentrate on the dolls which she though had the most immediate appeal and would cost the least to make. Her meeting at the BBC came straight after her trade show and she had little time to prepare. 'I just didn't know what my pitch was. Everything happened so quickly that I hadn't had time to think, and then suddenly all I knew was that I was going into the Den and being confronted by those five Dragons.'

Filming for the show starts at seven in the morning, so entrepreneurs are put up in a hotel the night before. Sarah didn't turn up at the hotel until 11 pm, but before morning she had learned how to use Excel. 'I knew nothing. I didn't even know what net profit and gross profit were.' Christine, her business mentor, sat up with her until 2 am going through the figures. 'I had to memorise them for the whole day. I was absolutely terrified.'

Originally, Christine was going to come into the Den too, as Sarah's business advocate, but she had to go into hospital on the day itself, so Sarah had to face the Dragons alone. 'I'm standing there thinking, where's Christine? I can't believe she's left me! But it all worked out in the end.'

Sarah asked the Dragons for a £35,000 investment in return for 20 per cent equity. She explained the Youdoo Doll, how it was a small, homemade rag doll that could be personalised with transfer papers using a computer, printer and scanner to create a 'mini-me'. The doll came in a box with clothing as well as the transfer papers, but Sarah also explained about the on-line fashion boutique she'd created where you could buy add-ons for the doll. To bring the idea to life, Sarah presented each Dragon with their own personalised doll, which caused considerable distraction!

The Dragons were interested and amused, but Duncan Bannatyne was horrified to discover that the dolls retailed at £19.99. 'Are you joking?' he exclaimed. However, he seemed impressed by her early sales figures – 800 in 3 and a half weeks, with a fresh order for 200 – and by her high-profile customers, like Top Shop. The attention of the other Dragons was captured, too. James

Caan asked how much the dolls cost to make. Sarah could not suppress a giggle as she told him, 'At the moment they're being made at home for £5.71, by my auntie and family and friends.' James suggested that if she ordered the packaging from China or Taiwan, instead of using a local manufacturer, she could cut costs considerably.

Deborah Meaden was intrigued by the dolls, but saw them as a gimmick with a very limited shelf life. 'The fact that these will appeal to creative people who have a pretty low boredom threshold, they are going to want to know what happens next.' Sarah thought that by the end of the third year any investor would double their money, but Deborah wasn't so sure they'd last that long: 'I think that by year three, this will be done and dusted.' Sarah defended herself by explaining that she intended to create a brand – 'There could be lots of variations. We've got "Valentine's Day", we've got "Father's Day" … I want to make your own, "girl band" and "boy band" – that kind of thing.'

Theo Paphitis was less impressed than Sarah had expected. As a retailer, he said, he thought the dolls would use up too much wall space. 'The packaging should be half that size, and actually the quality's rubbish. It really is amateur time.' Sarah countered, 'It's meant to look homemade,' but Theo was scathing. 'Trust me – it works,' he said dismissively. 'Those are the reasons I can't back you. So "I'm out".'

Peter Jones quickly followed suit. 'I think this is *fun*,' he said, 'but with the expense of sorting out the things Theo's pointed out, the £35,000 will go pretty rapidly and that's the reason why I wouldn't invest in you, so "I'm out".'

Outwardly, Sarah remained calm and polite, but inside she was panicking as her creation was rubbished and her chances of winning backing were slipping away. Deborah Meaden shared Theo's concerns, and reiterated that she thought the dolls would be a 'One-Christmas wonder.' It looked as though she, too, would turn her back. But to Sarah's surprise she made an offer. 'I'm going to need a healthy chunk of the business … I'm going to offer you £35,000 and I want 45 per cent.'

James Caan declared his hand. 'I'd like to offer you the whole amount for 40 per cent of the equity. I think you don't need any help at all – I think you're doing a great job.'

It was still possible that the last Dragon, Duncan Bannatyne, would undercut the competition, but instead he withdrew. So now Sarah was faced with a choice. Should she sacrifice a larger stake in the business in return for Deborah's support and advice, or would she be tempted by James Caan's more 'hands off' approach?

Deborah's opinion is that Sarah has 'very good instincts'. Her instinct now was to go with the offer that promised more support – a wise decision, considering how much she'd relied on Christine in the past. She accepted Deborah's offer, and left the Den in a daze. 'My brain went completely blank. I felt really spaced out. I didn't tell my mum until the next day. I just had to deal with it on my own first.' Sarah had made her presentation wearing a skimpy, customised T-shirt ('as an artist, I always want to look different') and low-cut jeans. When she finally told her mother – 'She panicked because my family didn't know about my tattoos. That was her main concern. "We'll just pretend that it washes off!"'

Deborah started working with Sarah Lu almost immediately. 'We really had to go for the Christmas market. I put Sarah Lu on to a manufacturer who will do all the fulfilling, so that Sarah can be left in the creative space. And Christmas was excellent. Our website had so many hits, we were actually listed as the toy most likely to succeed over Christmas. Chris Evans mentioned it on his show, so did Jonathan Ross – there was a lot of buzz around it.'

Since *Dragons' Den*, Sarah has been working 24/7. 'I nearly didn't go home for Christmas.' Deborah feels strongly that Youdoo Doll has got to keep moving, and Sarah has been creating a product range. 'A twelve-year-old schoolboy Facebooked me saying "I want to stick my sister's face on a cow!" I'm working on a Youdoo pet. It should be quite funny.'

She's delighted, though surprised, to find herself working with Deborah. 'I didn't really expect it to be Deborah. But I thought it would be nice to get her on board because she's a girl as well. I thought, girl power would be good!' And so it has proved to be. 'We call each other every week. I've always taken plenty of risks, but working with Deborah I feel safer.' Deborah is equally enthusiastic. 'She's very, very responsive is Sarah Lu. She's energetic and quick-thinking. She knows more than she thinks she knows.'

Despite the workload, Sarah Lu is enjoying post-Den life. 'I've been asked to do talks at colleges and universities round the country. And I think the nicest part is the emails I get from people saying I've really inspired them. One was from a girl doing business studies who said, "Every time we think of entrepreneurs we think of Richard Branson, and now we're thinking of you." And that's really, really, really nice.'

A LESSON IN MAKING THE WEB WORK FOR YOU:
EMMIE MATTHEWS AND ED STEVENS' GAMING ALERTS

Gaming Alerts was set up by Emmie Matthews and Ed Stevens to deliver up-to-date offers, information and the latest odds direct to the PCs of gamblers interested in on-line bingo, poker, casinos and sports betting. Users select their interests and Gaming Alerts provides tailored information to fit their criteria. Like websites such as confuse.com or moneysupermarket.com, Gaming Alerts makes money by referring customers to other relevant sites in exchange for commission.

Emmie and Ed are, as they put it, 'good mates' who met through work and have friends in common – Emmie knows Ed's wife and goes out with one of his best friends. The idea of a comparison gaming site originated with Emmie. The concept behind it was similar to the BBC News or Sky News alerts, but Gaming Alerts would tip off people who wanted to play poker or bingo. Emmie had worked for a company that created the technology for on-line desktop alerts and believed it could be developed for gambling on-line. They had both worked in on-line gaming and understood the growth opportunities for the business as a whole.

Ed and Emmie had already set up one successful affiliate

marketing business called Jack Media London. They had a small team of ten people working with them, and understood the process of running a business. They admit that when they started 'Jacks' they didn't write a business plan – they just left their jobs and began the company without much preparation. Gaming Alerts would need to be handled differently, as it would be expensive to create as a start-up. First they needed to be certain that it was an unmet niche business opportunity, so they used the profits from Jack to run a small two-month pilot. It proved that there was definitely potential, but they would need an investor with deep pockets to take the idea forward.

Emmie, who studied economics and accounting at university, was used to working with the accountants and looking after the staff. She describes Ed as 'a typical bloke – brilliant at all the new business.' Between them, they had experience, technology, and research evidence ... but they needed an investment of £200,000 to get the business up and running.

As a great fan of *Dragons' Den*, Emmie thought it might be a perfect opportunity for Gaming Alerts, but it was only when the programme makers called that she admitted to Ed that she had put in an application. 'He wasn't very keen on the idea because he thought that if we didn't do very well it could damage our company.' After persuading Ed to audition, the next hurdle was the editorial policy at the BBC. Was gambling a suitable subject for the family audience of *Dragons' Den*? Emmie and Ed argued that, with over 7 per cent of the population in the UK gambling on-line (not counting those who play the National Lottery) and 3 million playing bingo in bingo halls, it was not a taboo subject any more. They pointed out that on-line gambling is heavily regulated: the government has put measures in place to protect the vulnerable, with restrictions on who can advertise, how they can advertise and what they can say in their adverts. With that obstacle overcome, they were in!

On the day of the TV recording, Emmie, not a morning person, got up at the crack of dawn and Ed drove them to the Den, arriving much too early. The first entrepreneurs to arrive, they were also the last to pitch, so they had a very long wait in the green room before it was their turn to appear.

Emmie said: 'Ed was going crazy. It's such a small, enclosed space and you're not allowed out because they don't want you to see the Dragons or the other entrepreneurs coming back. Eventually we got called in. We were pretty nervous when we got upstairs because it was very hot. You're surrounded by bright lights, and then you find these five Dragons staring at you.'

Theo Paphitis takes up the story:

'As people walk into the Den, sometimes you see a sparkle in their eyes, and with Ed and Emmie you could see the lights were on. Life is about timing, and the timing was absolutely spot on.'

Theo's much-loved wife, Mrs P, is what he calls a 'bingoholic'. She plays on-line a great deal, and not only did Theo understand the on-line gaming community because of her interest, he had also once owned a bingo hall and more recently had researched on-line gaming and affiliate sites. He understood how they work in retailing and marketing. But he was keen to keep his knowledge of the gaming sector to himself, because he didn't want the other Dragons to know he thought Ed and Emmie had a great proposal. He planned to keep quiet and listen. However, as Duncan Bannatyne was aggressively questioning Ed and Emmie on their financial projections, and was completely incredulous at the thought of people sitting at home playing bingo, Theo had to reveal his interest:

'OK, stop there please, because you're about to insult Mrs P. She plays bingo on-line every single night.'

He was ready to invest. Poor Ed and Emmie did not know this, and all they could see was the Dragons turning to them and saying, 'I'm out'. Emmie was trying to stay calm while Ed was muttering, 'I told you this would happen,' and 'This is going to be a disaster.' Emmie had always liked Deborah Meaden on the programme and was very hopeful that she might invest, so it was a serious blow when she said no. But Emmie and Ed understood how investing in their business would be hard for anyone who did not have direct experience of the on-line gambling world: 'If you don't know people that gamble on-line, you probably don't understand the potential for investing in a company like ours,' said Emmie. But it was a blow not to have the support of those two.

Only Theo remained and at last he showed his hand. He wanted to invest, but not on the terms they were offering: 'I would love to invest in you two – seriously. I'm desperately trying to find ways in which it makes sound, economic, commercial sense. So I'm going to give you one chance to come up with something that might tempt me to make this more commercial, because £200,000 for 10 per cent is nowhere near.'

After some tough negotiation Emmie and Ed eventually offered 30 per cent of their company in return for the money they desperately needed to get their business off the ground.

Since celebrating the deal with champagne in Theo's office and banking the £200,000, Emmie and Ed have been working with Theo on future plans for Gaming Alerts – improving design, building new websites and targeting other western European countries. They have journalists writing news content for the site and a tipster on the sports betting website. They are working on ensuring that the user experience on the site is good. In the longer term they will provide news, information and forums and try to build a real community around the Gaming Alerts site. Theo has invited them to move into his London offices.

'It's not often that you come across two such bright individuals, and whilst £200,000 is a huge amount of my children's inheritance, if I was going to invest it in anybody, I was going to invest it in Emmie and Ed. It's very, very hard to find new young talent that's hungry and understands where it's going. I'm not saying they are perfect. None of us are. There were quite a few things that we've had to look at again and to be quite firm about, but they listen, and if the point is valid they take it on board very readily.'

Surprisingly, Theo admits that one of the reasons he wants to spend more time with Emmie and Ed is that although they are learning from him about marketing, he is also learning a great deal from them.

'I'm getting an education. I've paid a lot of money for it, but now we have a business that's generating money that I feel very pleased about. I'm looking forward to a very close and prosperous relationship.'

A LESSON IN EXPLOITING THE MARKET:
PETER MOULE AND CHOCBOX

Most people go into the Dragons' Den looking for a cash investment. Peter Moule was different. He did not need the Dragons' money, but their time and expertise. He already had a successful business supplying electricians, but believed there could be many new customers if the Dragons would help him.

As a child, Peter always wanted to know how things worked: he was always dismantling them and putting them back together. He says, 'I was always full of ideas. I wanted to be an inventor.' His family wasn't affluent. 'Like most people in Haringey we lived in a flat. We were on the ground floor and Mum and Dad and my brother and I all slept in the front room. My nan had the back bedroom, and there was just a scullery and a living room. We used to wash in a tin bath. The people who lived above us had to walk through our flat to go upstairs to theirs.'

Now, Peter is a millionaire.

He inherited his entrepreneurial spirit from his parents – his father was a technical director and his mother had a wool shop. It was his mother who taught him what he believes are the basics of business: 'If you can't pay your bills this month, you'll never pay them next month,' and 'Don't have something you can't afford.'

When his parents set up an electrical contracting business his mother did the bookwork and made sure that suppliers were paid on time: 'All the other companies would make electricians wait for their money but she'd send them a cheque by return. We always had a good reputation, not only with the clients but also with all the workers, which meant that they would do us favours they wouldn't do for other companies.' Treating workers well has been an ethos that Peter has always followed and he thinks it helped to ensure his business success.

Peter was a fully qualified electrician. He moved into computer technology 'because I'm quite logical,' and then into computer sales, which he found he was good at. Eventually he joined the successful family company Bill Moule and Sons, installing electrics for exhibitions and displays. New regulations were introduced restricting the use of tape on electrical connections. Until then an electrician would use a connector strip to join wires and then wrap the connection in tape. The new rules decreed that the junction must be enclosed in a rigid case.

Peter says, 'I couldn't find anything specifically for connectors – so I invented something myself.' And the name? 'Electricians call the connector a "chocolate block connector strip," because it comes in a strip of twelve and you break off chunks of three, like a bar of chocolate. So I came up with the Chocbox.'

Peter contacted a plastics company and developed a design to take the Chocbox into production in the UK. He started to sell to the exhibition industry, and soon afterwards the Lighting

Association directed everyone participating in its major annual lighting show to use the Chocbox on all their lights. Then B&Q stores caught on, fitting Chocboxes in all their lighting aisles. The business was taking off .

Peter was selling more than a million Chocboxes a year to electricians, but he thought the market could be larger: 'There are 36 million households in the UK. We were already selling a million a year to the trade, but if every household bought one, that would give me an extra million a year for the next thirty five years.'

At a business show Peter and his brother, 'after a few drinks', visited the *Dragons' Den* stand and 'had a bit of a laugh'. Two days later he received a call from the programme telling him to make a proper pitch and he was chosen to go on the show. Peter's wife wrote him a script for his pitch and he set off to the Den to meet the Dragons.

Peter's attitude was casual compared to the other entrepreneurs – after all, he already had a business that was doing well, and he was confident in his product. But waiting around before the recording he found his mouth getting dry. 'It's very cloak and dagger: you're stuck in the green room and even if you want to go to the toilet, somebody goes and waits outside. You mustn't have any contact with the Dragons. By the time I did my pitch I was very nervous.'

Peter was looking for an investment of £150,000 for 10 per cent equity in his company. He said that he was confident that, with the Dragons' expertise, in 3 years' time he could be selling more than 6 million units a year and making a profit in excess of £1.5 million.

Duncan Bannatyne revealed the Dragons' first impression of Peter: 'When he first came in front of us he looked a bit of a wide boy with his pinstripe suit and his glasses stuck on his head and we said "second-hand-car salesman".'

Theo Paphitis was not impressed that Peter had broken one of the basic rules of business by failing to protect his idea with an international patent. As James Caan put it:

'I'm just staggered. Why wouldn't it have dawned on you to register it in a much wider territory?'

Theo and Peter Jones declared themselves out and it was beginning to look as though it was all going badly wrong for Peter. But he was determined to secure the Dragons' expertise and made them an offer he hoped they couldn't refuse – a 'money-back guarantee' on any investment in him. Duncan Bannatyne was impressed and made his own offer.

'I think there might be an opportunity here for someone to invest in this and make a return. So, I'll give you an offer of £75,000 for 25 per cent and I will also give you an offer of £150,000 for 50 per cent of the company.'

Looking back, Duncan says that what attracted him was Peter's phenomenal belief in his product. But Deborah Meaden was suspicious: 'If something looks too good to be true, it's usually too good to be true.' She felt she would be wasting her time and pulled out.

Fortunately James was keen to invest. 'I'm going to give you the benefit of the doubt. I think you could have two Dragons rather than one. I'll certainly match Duncan's £75,000 and I'm happy to take not 25 but 22.5 per cent.

However, this would mean surrendering nearly half of his company, so Peter tried to get them to bring down their combined offer to a 30 per cent equity stake. After some intense negotiation he got the £150,000 investment in an equity deal that will come down to 36 per cent of the business after 3 years if agreed targets are reached. But, more importantly for him, he has two Dragons to help him to grow his business. As far as Duncan was concerned, his investment was a 'no brainer' – the company was worth what he was investing, so he couldn't lose his money!

Peter was in two minds when he left the Den – he went home and celebrated, but he didn't know whether he had done the right thing. But with the Dragons' help the business began to move forward. Through a good friend, James had a contact in GET, a worldwide electrical wholesaler selling 800,000 connecting strips a year in the UK, and the Chocbox fitted into their portfolio perfectly. With James's help, an exclusive distribution deal was negotiated. Assuming sales of 5 million units a year over the next 5 years, retailing at 99p, the business could reach £25 million, but Peter thinks that annual sales of 100 million are possible.

'In the UK, 15 million connector strips are sold every year, and each of those could use 4 Chocboxes, so we're talking 60 million units annually in this country alone,' he said. And GET has international distribution rights to the Chocbox in the 152 countries it supplies.

Peter also made a 'ratchet deal' with James and Duncan which means he will get 6 per cent of his business back from them if they make £1 million profit in any of the first 3 years.

So Chocbox is a growing business, but although Peter is on his way to becoming a multi-millionaire, he is a still an inventor at heart – 'I've got another invention, another type of electrical product. I can't say too much because we've got to get some intellectual property protection, but it's working and ready to roll.'

What's more, with James Caan, he is now helping others to develop their business; James has involved Peter with his investment business to interview prospective entrepreneurs looking at new ideas in the building trade.

Duncan, a 'people person', is delighted; 'Peter's a really nice guy and I'm glad he's making a success because I do like him.' Moreover, his instinct about the kind of person who makes a good investment prospect is giving him a fantastic return on this particular investment. 'The distribution company are doing all the work, so I shall really be sitting back now and just letting it happen. It's probably the most astute investment I've made in the Dragons' Den so far.'

A LESSON IN CASH FLOW:
SAMMY FRENCH AND FIT-FUR-LIFE

Sammy French had developed a canine treadmill to help keep dogs fit, and to aid their rehabilitation after injuries and operations. She arrived in the Den with her dog Daffy to show the Dragons how her Fit-Fur-Life treadmill operated, but although the Dragons were taken with her invention, they were less than impressed by her business management. Sammy desperately needed an investment from them to keep the business operating.

Sammy has always loved animals. She grew up on a 40-acre farm, mucking out stables at 6 am before school. Whenever animals needed special care, her father, a vet, would give them to Sammy to look after. Before she had her family she trained as an animal welfare photographer. Animals were a major part of her life. Now she is a single mother with an eight-year-old daughter and a seven-year-old son. When her former husband left her she decided that she didn't want to end up as a single parent living on benefits so, starting with two puppies, she began training dogs to provide an income for her family. The first dogs she had trained were her parents' Labrador puppies: 'You have to be very clear with your praise and with saying "no" – as long as you set very distinct boundaries with dogs, they love it.'

She began to think of new ways to get dogs fit without having to spend so many hours walking them. This became a more urgent consideration when an operation left her temporarily unable to walk. While she was recuperating she exercised by walking on a treadmill. 'That's when I put the dogs on my treadmill, but a human treadmill isn't really suitable for dogs. I thought there must be a way of adapting the idea for dogs, so I created my first plan for a treadmill for dogs.'

Sammy needed to get the canine treadmill produced. She found human fitness equipment manufacturers on the internet and after several approaches a company expressed interest in her idea. But they did not give her much input in the design of the product and although the model they manufactured functioned as a dog tread-mill, it was not of the quality that she wanted. However, it was sufficient to prove that there was a demand for the product.

Sammy became a retailer and spent two years exhibiting the dog treadmills but making very little profit. It was frustrating because the treadmill wholesaler would not let her alter the design or change factories – in their view the dog treadmill functioned satis-factorily. Sammy wanted more: she was still having to train dogs to make a living for her family while trying to get her company Fit-Fur-Life up and running, but she needed a backer. Her mother suggested she apply to *Dragons' Den*, but Sammy had not seen the programme in full, and she thought that the few parts she had glimpsed seemed very tough on the entrepreneurs. She did not want to put herself through a difficult ordeal. Instead of applying to the Den she sold the van she had been using to transport treadmills and with the money she flew to Taiwan to source manufacturers. After six days spent investigating factories with the help of a local agent, she chose two different firms to produce the first sample machine to her design and specification. Having two potential suppliers made good business sense because she could choose the most efficiently produced and highest quality treadmill. But time was running out. Would the treadmill be ready for Sammy's pre-booked exhibition space at the next Crufts Dog Show? Fortunately one supplier was able to deliver the goods: the new dog treadmill arrived in the UK just four days before Crufts. It generated a huge response and Sammy took 24 orders.

But this was when things began to go wrong. Sammy was unable to pay for the tooling and production of the machines to fulfill the orders she had taken. She considered either going into administration or using half of the money from the orders to pay for the tooling. She had paid for all the moulds and to start production she needed a further £16,000. She tried unsuccessfully to borrow from friends and was unable to use her council house as equity for a bank. She had orders to fulfil but no treadmills. Sammy was desperate. 'I thought if we could get into production I could continue getting more orders so that the money would be there to pay for the treadmills when they arrived. I know it wasn't logical but I'm not business-minded. I desperately needed an investor. I was working in a pub as a waitress to make ends meet. That was the moment to apply to *Dragons' Den*.'

Sammy was invited for an interview and two weeks later she was waiting to go into the Den. Waiting with her was Daffy, her dog, ready to demonstrate the Fit-Fur-Life treadmill to the Dragons.

'I was taken straight down to the Den, and didn't have the awful experience of sitting in the green room not knowing if you're actually going to pitch. Daffy was cuddled by every member of the production company, so he was feeling very laid back and just got on the treadmill and did his stuff.'

But for Sammy it was not so easy. She admits that she was very nervous. Although she had confidence in Daffy's part of the presentation and in her product she was worried that if the Dragons started delving into the position of the business, she might lose what she knew was her last chance to find the funds she needed to keep the business going.

Sammy asked for £100,000 for 25 per cent of her business. She pointed out that there was a large market for her treadmill: over 200,000 people train dogs in the professional industry such as vets and the police force; kennels and rescue centres would find her treadmill invaluable; and in the UK there are a further 5 million people who either own or work with dogs. She demonstrated the finely adjustable incline and decline features of the treadmill, and told the Dragons:

'I've tested this market with a previous model and I've sold 147 units. I am having to turn away business, because I simply cannot supply the demand for the product at this stage. What I would like to do with any investment is to finance the production run of the first 150 machines and then the sales generated from that will fully capitalise all the working requirements of the company and any future stock.'

At first the Den experience did not go well – Peter Jones said he thought 'it will be a sad day when we see a sort of dog gym.' Sammy was surprised because although she had heard similar comments when she started her business, she thought that this was an outdated attitude. However, Peter seemed impressed by the 300 per cent mark-up that Sammy was achieving. But Deborah Meaden was investigating the figures. When she heard Sammy's confession of just how serious her cash-flow problems were, and how she had failed to get a cash injection from the bank, Deborah looked shocked. Sammy's pitch was in real trouble. Peter had heard enough, he was out. Then came a tough analysis from Deborah.

'Sammy, I don't think I can invest in somebody when halfway through their presentation I've had to say, "Can you please come clean?" If you'd stood here and said frankly "I'm in dire straits but I've got a great product" it probably would have happened, because I like frankness. What worries me most is that your reputation's shot. You've already failed to deliver 24 machines, so I'm afraid I'm out.'

Sammy was very upset at Deborah's comments. As far as she was concerned she was doing everything possible. She could have put the company into administration, but instead she was battling on to try to make it work and to fulfil the orders she already had. But to her great relief James Caan was still listening. James was carefully observing Sammy and thinking, 'Here's a woman who needs to be given an opportunity. She's clearly demonstrated that she's prepared to make an effort.' He recognised that business was not Sammy's strength but that wasn't unusual in somebody who has never been in business before, who essentially is a mother busy bringing up her children. He thought that he could give her the confidence to go out and pitch to bigger customers.

'I suppose I just wanted to give her the opportunity and the support – to give her the capital to be able to create a future for her and her family.'

He said, 'I'll offer you the £100,000 you're looking for, but I think I'd want 50 per cent in order to take that risk.'

The other Dragons encouraged Sammy to take James's money – Theo said, 'It's a great offer. Bite his arm off.' And so Sammy accepted.

While Sammy and Daffy were being interviewed by the programme's host, Evan Davis, James was patiently waiting outside in the rain to speak to Sammy. 'All that time, he was waiting for me, bless him, and he shook my hand and said "Can you drop me an email this afternoon, and let's get cracking on this."'

She points out that even after her successful session in the Den, it was still a stressful time after the programme. While James was carrying out due diligence on her company, she was dealing with her customers and waiting to go into production. But eventually the deal was completed and she has now spent the £100,000 from James on new treadmills. James says the first thing they did was to fly her to Taiwan to meet the manufacturers to make sure that she got the product absolutely perfect in its testing, durability and technical capability. The treadmills are arriving in the UK and Sammy is attending more exhibitions and shows to create more sales. Now that she can offer a high-end product that generates revenue for businesses that care for dogs in rehabilitation she can attend shows specifically for veterinary surgeons. James has put her in contact with the Guide Dogs for the Blind Association, which has five and a half thousand seeing-eye dogs. He also wants her to approach his contacts in the Army and the Police, selling to the corporate market rather than to individuals. As he says: 'Suddenly everything's happening.'

So what does she think of James? 'He's fantastic, he's put in a brilliant team of people around me and we've worked very hard – hopefully 2008 will start to show the rewards.' Sammy now has a business partner to turn to: 'If I have any problems business-wise that I wouldn't have been able to deal with before, now I can just phone James or one of his team and they help me to handle it. He's been so helpful making contracts and all that kind of thing which I've never done before.' Now Sammy has what she calls 'a proper business', with many different companies wanting to sell the treadmills and in the long run she aims to move from retailing the treadmills herself to providing them as a wholesaler.

Meanwhile, she is run off her feet. 'A lot of people want my time, they want to see me, they want to introduce their dogs, they want me to come and talk to them about Fit-Fur-Life.' She has been receiving international enquiries and believes that the dog treadmill market has huge potential worldwide – and she already has a new design in her head for a cat treadmill. 'I think this will keep me busy for a few years yet.'

A LESSON IN BUILDING BUSINESS AROUND AN INDIVIDUAL:
LABAN ROOMES AND MIDAS TOUCH

Midas Touch, now known as Goldgenie, offers custom gold-plating for a wide variety of items, from phones to MP3 players to fixtures and fittings to car emblems. The gold-plating machine is portable so work can conveniently be carried out on site. Laban Roomes formed Midas Touch in 1995. Twelve successful years later he pitched his product on Dragons' Den *in an attempt to finance his growing franchise business. Laban's triumph in the Den was testament to a strong, resourceful personality that impressed all five of the Dragons.*

Laban describes his childhood as 'beautiful', citing a very close relationship with his mother. Yet it was far from easy. She told him when he was eleven that she could not afford to buy him new clothes. To make up the shortfall, Laban began selling custard creams at school, but soon set up a hedge-cutting business that rapidly diversified into more general gardening. His earnings quickly outstripped his mother's. 'I bought Mum a colour TV, we decorated her whole house, we got a telephone for the first time. We had this beautiful relationship where she was my mother but she was also my business partner.'

Leaving school at 15 with just two CSEs, Laban never settled until at 18 he set up his next business, Fancy Promotions, where people would pay £2 to enter stories they had written into a competition to win cash prizes. 'My mother's side of the family in Jamaica lived in abject poverty and I thought, right, what can I do to help? So I used the profits to buy and export Lada cars.' Eventually, Laban established a number of taxi routes between Kingston and May Pen.

Laban's experience was enriched by a period in the 1980s of organising raves. 'We'd hold these acid parties in fields where we made an amazing amount of money. I paid off my mother's house and we invested more money into the cars in Jamaica.'

Laban's next unpredictable step was to become a social worker at a refuge set up by Princess Diana. Interviewing children who had been abused, though, was difficult for someone who had two children of his own: 'I found it disturbing and very distressing for me as a young person, so I decided to leave and focus on my business in Jamaica.' Heartbreakingly, he discovered that the company had failed and at the same time he received a call from home telling him that his mother, who sometimes suffered from mental illness, had fallen ill again. The accumulated pressure caused a split between Laban and his girlfriend.

Laban felt that he had lost everything. It was a friend that introduced him to the gold-plating business. Laban saw the product in America and, with the help of a loan from his ex-girlfriend, he designed a prototype for a portable gold-plating machine himself.

'It fitted with me as an individual, my character, a young black guy who used to wear gold and diamond rings.'

'I built up the business from my friend's floor where I was sleeping. I literally walked around with the machine on my back. I built up an amazing business with Lexus car dealerships. I'd wake up in the morning and drive to Manchester, then to Birmingham, then back down to Milton Keynes. I'd research each area and tell them that I was local because I didn't want them to think I was a one-man band.'

With encouragement from a friend, Laban passed a screen test to appear on *Dragons' Den*, yet on two separate occasions, Laban pulled out at the very last moment. 'I made 101 excuses to myself, like: I'm too good for them; I don't want these strangers in my company; I can do it without them.'

Finally, a chance encounter with *Dragons' Den* legend Levi Roots, the man who made a nationwide splash with his Reggae Reggae Sauce, changed his mind. Levi encouraged Laban to grab the opportunity. 'I realised that I had been fearful of maybe not succeeding, of maybe making a fool of myself.' Soon after, Laban was devastated to discover that a great friend had been found dead and, acknowledging the unpredictability of life, he took the plunge.

'When I arrived I was very, very nervous, but I just focused on the present. It calmed me down and I think it was that thinking that enabled me to win. I remember just focusing on getting to the door and then getting up those stairs, taking each task individually.' With five minutes to go an assistant producer asked why he was so calm. 'I started talking to her about my friend and halfway through the story I started to cry really hard. The clock was counting down with about two minutes to go and I started to cry a river.' Fortunately, Laban was able to compose himself in time to face the Dragons.

An effectively simple pitch demonstrated how the portable gold-plating machine worked and Laban doled out examples of gold-plated iPods, mobile phones and flowers. He asked for £60,000 to help expand his franchise business in return for a 20 per cent share in the company.

Theo Paphitis elicited from Laban that the cost of the franchise was £10,000 plus VAT. Laban seemed relaxed, modest, yet confident, yet within seconds his careful pitch began to unravel as he briefly confused turnover with profit and this unintentional error seemed to throw him off balance. Responding to Theo's probing, he claimed that the annual profit for a franchisee was a tiny £10,000.

Next he told Deborah Meaden that the real annual profit figure was £35,000, admitting that his figures were 'jumbled in his head'. Deborah lost her patience: 'Laban, I don't want this to be happening. This is the absolute, most important number or fact that you had to come in with. How much is a franchisee going to earn? It's one number.' In addition, Deborah was not convinced that most people possessed Laban's ability to put in the hard graft he'd achieved and she dropped out of the running.

At Theo's prompting, Laban expounded on his incredible life's journey, but although it induced obvious admiration, it was not enough for Duncan Bannatyne: 'Laban, I think you're an inspiration. You're very good at what you do. The trouble is, making that into a business that can be at all scaleable is very difficult because the profit isn't much more than making a really good living.'

Theo believed that Laban needed more than £60,000 to establish the business and failed to see how he could gain a return. Peter Jones was generous, but also unwilling to flash the cash: 'People like dealing with you, you're an engaging individual. But you need to go and find another 30 Labans and I think you might struggle.'

All of which left James Caan. James was positive, but with reservations: 'I like anything that sparkles. But I think you're a long way from having a structured developed proposition that can be replicated the way that you want.' Sensing hope, Laban passionately detailed the work he had done at Neasden Temple and emphasised a Hollywood connection through the Emmy Awards. Thankfully, James offered the full £60,000 but in return for 40 per cent of the business, warning: 'It's conditional upon you and I agreeing where we are going to invest that money.'

'I was impressed by Laban's spirit, by his tremendous character and drive that he has displayed throughout his life,' reveals James. 'I could see that he was already a success and that he would continue to be a success regardless of any investment and that was encouraging. He had never had help before because he did not necessarily need it. I respected that, because I started my own working life in a similar way.' James is an investor extremely interested in the individual, perhaps above and beyond the idea or the state of a business. As someone who refused to take a perceived easier route in his working life by spurning the family business perhaps he felt an affinity with Laban's extraordinary entrepreneurial spirit.

Laban has been delighted with the subsequent results: 'To date I've only used £25,000 of the £60,000 and I probably won't use any more because the business is making money. He advised me to build up the internet side and to get people doing the gold-plating for me. It has enabled me to excel because I've always been too involved in the hands-on work myself. We've also moved the business to Hatton Garden. That was one of James's first things. If you're going to buy a suit, you think about Savile Row. If you're going to buy gold, you go to Hatton Garden.'

Laban's products can now be found in Harrods – a dream come true: 'On the second floor they're selling our gold plated flowers and golf balls and putters and on the third floor it's our gold plated iPods. We've also done a deal with Selfridges.' The relationship with James has been both close and beneficial: 'We had a fantastic first meeting at his house. Now I liken myself to a Premiership footballer – I'm scoring goals, so James does have time for me. We probably meet at least once every two weeks.'

Laban's advice, similar to many entrepreneurs, is to find a business that suits you: 'I think when you go into business you've got to try and look at your character and try and get something that can fit with that. I loved this business because it was flexible and it had a kind of mystique.'

EPILOGUE

So there you have it. Stories of success, stories of failure, lessons learnt the hard way, deals done, investments flourishing and profit made.

The stories in *Dragons' Den: Success From Pitch To Profit* show that you too can be successful if you do your homework, know your business inside out and have that elusive something extra.

But be warned. Not everyone makes it, for every success there are many failures. Use the advice of the Dragons, learn from the entrepreneurs who have braved the Den and understand Evan Davis's rules of economics. With these tools you can embark on a journey from pitch to profit.

INDEX